HISTORIC TREASURES OF NEW HAVEN

CELEBRATING 375 YEARS OF THE ELM CITY

LAURA A. MACALUSO

Charleston   London

THE
History
PRESS

Published by The History Press
Charleston, SC 29403
www.historypress.net

Copyright © 2013 by Laura A. Macaluso
All rights reserved

Cover images: Front: top left courtesy of the Athletic Department, Yale University; top right courtesy of the Jewish Historical Society of Greater New Haven; middle courtesy of the Owl Shop; lower right courtesy of the Eli Whitney Museum; and lower left courtesy of the Connecticut Ukrainian American Historical Society. All photography by Jessica Zielonka. Back: top left courtesy of Laura A. Macaluso; top right courtesy of the Irving S. Gilmore Music Library, Yale University; middle courtesy of Joseph Taylor; bottom courtesy of the Yale University Art Gallery.

First published 2013

Manufactured in the United States

ISBN 978.1.60949.771.2

Library of Congress CIP data applied for.

This book is for my parents, Paul and Alexandra Macaluso,
who always liked old stuff

and

"Respectfully dedicated to the Citizens of New Haven"
(from the "Plan of the Town of New Haven," C. Currier, 1748)

Little girl waving on the New Haven Green, surrounded by markers and banners for the tercentenary celebration, circa 1938. *Courtesy of Joseph Taylor.*

"The Birth of New-Haven"

A new Song, written and sung by Mr. Wm. Goodwin, at the celebration
of the Two Hundredth Anniversary of the settlement of the Town and
Colony of New Haven, April 25, 1838.

Tune: "Poor Old Robinson Crusoe"

By subscription I took
A useful neat book,
Which produced has some pleasing reflections;
By writer so famed,
'Tis properly named
"Connecticut Historical Collections"
By Barber, the man for collections:
To each reader and friend
I would strong recommend
Barber's Historical Collections.

If to read you're inclined
On its pages you'll find,
Some men from Old England brought leaven.
When over safe got,
They touch'd on this spot,
And made a happy New Haven.
They one and all worked with their leaven,
To make them a home and New Haven;
They did staunch and straight,
In sixteen thirty-eight,
Make this their home and New Haven.

For twelve coats of English cloth
And spoons to sup broth,
Twelve hatchets, twelve hoes, and some leaven.
They bought this good land
On which we now stand,
And made it their splendid New Haven—
Ah! yes, it's a lovely New Haven.
They made famous use of their leaven,

Search all the world round,
None such can be found,
To equal our garden, New Haven.

The eighteenth, a good day
Of April, they say,
They ceased from their toils and were shaven;
With a cordial good greeting
They held their first meeting,
And prayed that their souls might be saven;
Good, happy and free,
They prayed they might be,
In their snug little harbor, New Haven.

They concocted sound laws,
With very few flaws,
And chose from their stock of prime leaven
A man that was good,
Who's perils withstood,
And Gov'nor made him of New Haven.
He proved a good choice from their leaven,
Did this Gov'nor elect of New Haven;
'Twas Eaton, sirs, he
Who lived to be free,
And Gov'nor of happy New Haven.

Whalley, Dixwell and Goffe,
From England ran off,
With consciences black as a raven,
Made this their abode
Through life's rugged road,

And atoned for their sins in New-Haven.
From their foes they escaped to New Haven,
And with many staunch friends in New Haven,
Their tombs may be seen
On the square that is green,
At the back of a church in New Haven.

Five hundred law books,
Full of matters and crooks,
Were sent to these men of the leaven;
Who read with surprise,
And made themselves wise,
And lawyers a batch for New-Haven,
Moulded they were from the leaven,
And became mighty men of New Haven;
By finding out flaws,
And using their jaws,
They rulers became of New-Haven.

To give men more knowledge,
Yale founded a college,
With professors worked out from the leaven;
To their credit redound,
Great scholars, profound,
Were made in the Yale of New Haven;
Ay! that is the place for prime leaven,
Learned men may be found in New-Haven.
May the college of Yale,
Nor its friends never fail,
But stand like a rock in New-Haven.

In eighteen thirty-two,
Fine churches no few,
Were built for the people to pray in,
'Tis pleasing to tell,
Supported they're well,
By folks that are good in New-Haven,
Yes, steady good souls of New-Haven,
That sprung from the old-fashioned leaven;
And ministers true
To the gospel, will you
Find in this garden, New-Haven.

A thousand things more,
Has this book, friends, in store,
Of those that have sprung from this leaven;
But, Sirs, I've not time,
More facts to enrhyme,
So must finish my song of New-Haven,
And pronounce it all good from the leaven,
Sure nothing can vie with New-Haven;
May God bless the race,
Who now fill the place,
Of the pilgrims that founded New-Haven.

–William Goodwin, **Daily Herald,**
April 27, 1838, vol. 6, no. 98.

CONTENTS

CONTENTS

PREFACE

The return of this anniversary will find all its late participants in the tomb; but if the solemnities and recollections of the occasion shall tend to keep alive the spirit of patriotism and love of New England's peculiar institutions, the festivities of its advent will prove a permanent blessing.
–Columbian Register, *New-Haven, April 28, 1838*

For more than two hundred years, New Haven has had a particular proclivity for marking the passage of time, creating celebrations that draw on the people, places and events unique to the Elm City. The inclination to mark anniversaries and other significant occasions is not unique in world history, past or present, east or west, north or south. The summer of 2012 comes easily to mind when remembering that Britons and many people around the world celebrated two bookend events with historical pageants of ribbons, medals and political, musical and athletic performances. The summer began with the one-thousand-vessel flotilla on the Thames (in appropriate English rain) to mark Queen Elizabeth II's Diamond Jubilee (or sixty years on the throne) and ended with American swimmer Michael Phelps weighted down with an astonishing career total of twenty-two medals—eighteen of them gold—at the XXX Olympiad. While not as important on the international stage, the Elm City has nevertheless set the pace for celebrating in the state, though the number and size of these events have lessened from their climax between 1850 and 1950.

New Haven's 375th anniversary in April 2013 is an opportunity to look back over the many celebrations that have taken place here and also to provide a framework for future planners in 2038, New Haven's quatercentenary. It is hard to imagine what that event will look like in 2038, let alone 2138, as Horace Day said at the turn of the nineteenth century:

> *The 25th day of April, A.D. 2138 will be a memorable day in New Haven. Five hundred years of the life of this community will then have passed away. No human wisdom can foresee what that day will witness. Controverted opinions settled, intellectual and moral culture assuming new forms, fresh discoveries made of the relations of the forces of nature may show that the men of to-day were as little capable of comprehending this future progress as the men of 1638 could comprehend what we now see to have been accomplished.*

This book is, in a sense, the history of an American culture that no longer exists. Collective society has been inextricably altered by technologies such as television (which made its first appearance in the New Haven tercentenary celebration in 1938) and its relations, the personal computer and Internet, all of which have opened up great vistas of communication and community but closed down others. Nevertheless, there is still a desire to mark milestones and special occasions, and in other areas of life, such as holidays, weddings and birthdays, these events have taken on increasingly larger roles in society. On the national stage, the years 2012–15 mark the 200th anniversary of the War of 1812, and 2011–15 marks the 150th anniversary of the Civil War, with the 150th anniversary of the Emancipation Proclamation receiving special attention in 2013. In New Haven, the years 2011–13 are a magnet for many milestone celebrations:

- New Haven Preservation Trust, 50th in 2011
- New Haven Museum, 150th in 2012–13
- *New Haven Register*, 200th in 2012
- New Haven Public Library, 125th in 2012
- New Haven Fire Department, 150th in 2012
- Lyric Hall, 100th in 2012
- Jewish Community Center of Greater New Haven, 100th in 2012
- Beinecke Rare Book and Manuscript Library, 50th in 2013
- Ethnic Heritage Center, 25th in 2013
- Connecticut Irish American Historical Society, 25th in 2013
- Blizzard of 1888, 125th in 2013
- Cole Porter at Yale, 100th in 2013

These are the organizations or events that give shape to New Haven life and culture. Without them and others, New Haven would be Anywhere Else, USA. Without them, writing New Haven history would be close to impossible. We need to recognize their contributions and/or support their work in every way possible. Celebrating New Haven's 375th year is the ideal opportunity to do just that.

My original plan for this book was to highlight 375 years of New Haven history by showcasing 375 historic objects. After all, there are lots of appealing objects in New Haven museums, libraries and archives, and books written about New Haven history have used objects as illustrations but not much more. Coincidentally, the *New York Times* ran an article, "A History of New York in 50 Objects," in the September 2, 2012 issue, and from here I discovered that Neil McGregor, the director of the British Museum, had published his *A History of the World in 100 Objects* in 2010. I began speaking with friends and colleagues and heard many ideas in return. Others were beginning to think about the 375th anniversary, too, and many envisioned using the opportunity to create community-based programs that combined some of the things New Haven is really good at—art and food usually topping the list. Margaret Bodell, Kim Futrell, Alan Plattus, Leland Torrance, Robert Greenberg, Andy Horowitz, Michael Rogers and Joe Taylor were some of these interested, friendly boosters, each of whom brings great things (artistic talent, creative community programming, historical awareness and more) to the Elm City. Thanks also to Steve Courtney and Sheila Levrant de Bretteville for their encouragement. Fortunately, Catherine Zipf, my advisor at Salve Regina University at the time, suggested that if I had a project that I wanted to see happen, the best thing to do was to "find a way to do it." Without interest from organizations, the larger ideas for community programming and grant writing fell away, and the core of my original idea, to talk about objects and New Haven history, was heard, thankfully, by The History Press.

Once I began researching the ways in which New Haven designed celebrations around milestones such as anniversaries, the task at hand shifted from selecting 375 wildly divergent objects through which to tell New Haven's story to crafting a mostly chronological narrative around significant celebrations in New Haven and the objects that were produced from them. Either way, the undertaking was enormous. Visiting many of New Haven's museums and collecting institutions within a three-month period and needing to look at objects meant that curators, collections managers, volunteers, directors, archivists and librarians needed to provide access to their exhibits, backrooms and files, often for more than one visit. These people work hard to ensure that New Haven history is preserved, and I thank each and every one and also offer my regrets if I have missed anyone who helped.

The following people were of great assistance to me during this project, and for this I am deeply grateful: Joan Cavanagh of the Ethnic Heritage Center and the Greater New Haven Labor History Association; Peter Vollemans of the Ethnic Heritage Center; Marvin Bargar, archivist of the Jewish Historical Society of Greater New Haven Inc.; Laura Parisi, president of the Italian American Historical Society of Connecticut; Geraldine Poole, archivist/librarian of the Greater New Haven African-American Historical Society; Pat Heslin, secretary of the Connecticut Irish American Historical Society; and Gloria Horbaty, president, and Irene Hladkyj, archivist, of the Connecticut Ukrainian American Historical Society.

At the New Haven Museum, I thank Jason Bischoff-Wurstle, Bonnie Campbell, James Campbell, Michelle Cheng, Katie Piascyk, Frances Skelton, Margaret Anne Tockarshewsky and Donna Wardle, all of whom have made great strides to redirect and reenergize an important New Haven institution. At the Institute Library, many thanks go to Executive Director William C. Baker and consulting curator Stephen Kobasa, both of whom are always a pleasure to talk to and who have also charged a waning New Haven organization with new energy, as well as a healthy respect for history. Mary Lou Cummings, curator/registrar at the Knights of Columbus Museum, and Bill Brown, director of the Eli Whitney Museum, were equally accessible, and their institutions, though different as night and day, tell stories intrinsic to New Haven and world history. Also, thanks to Christine Bertoni at the Peabody Essex Museum in Salem, Massachusetts.

In the realm of Yale University, I thank Richard Boursy, archivist, and Emily Ferrigno, public services assistant, of the Irving S. Gilmore Music Library. Conversations with Richard, via e-mail and in person, were one of the highlights of my time spent doing the legwork of this project. For every question I had, Richard could provide multiple sources and related ideas, and his holistic view of the "town/gown" relationship between New Haven and Yale was appreciated. William Purvis, Nicholas Renouf and Susan E. Thompson, curators of the Yale Collection of Musical Instruments, provided access to one of the few New Haven treasure houses that I had never been to before. Lea K. Cline, Coins and Medals Fellow; Jane Miller, museum assistant; and William E. Metcalf, Ben Lee Damsky Curator of Coins and Medals, Yale University Art Gallery, were great to assist me in the middle of their move to the exquisitely refurbished space in the Yale University Art Gallery. Nancy Franco, director of the Yale University Visitor Center, is always of great assistance. Barbara Narendra, archives and meteorites, and Patrick Sweeney, collections manager, Division of Botany of the Peabody Museum of Natural History, were my sources at that iconic museum. Thanks to Anthony "Duke" Diaz of the Yale University Athletic Department, for an insider's tour of Payne Whitney Gynmasium, and to Terry Dagradi, curator at the Cushing Center, Harvey Cushing/John Hay Whitney Medical Library, who is a pleasure to talk to (and I'm sorry that the fascinating collections under her care did not make it into the book). Also, thanks to Judith Schiff, chief research archivist, Sterling Memorial Library and the City of New Haven municipal historian, who is a resource beyond compare. Finally, many thanks to the Rights and Reproductions Department at the Yale University Art Gallery.

The mission of not-for-profit institutions like those mentioned here fit easily into the "contributes to the history of New Haven" category, but there are many other places, such as businesses and restaurants, that are part of a healthy mix of the past and present; their histories are deeply intertwined with the Elm City. Thanks to Elias Rodriguez, director of operations, East Rock Pharmacy; Glen Greenberg, owner of the Owl Shop; and Kenneth Adams, the general manager of Mory's. More than ever, in the midst of an ever altering downtown New Haven, these places need and deserve community support and patronage just like museums, archives and libraries because they contribute to the sense of place that makes New Haven distinctive.

Though the gathering of the content for this project was a considerable undertaking, the technical support for the creation of this work was critical. Fortunately, I have a resource who never fails to point me in the right direction: Camille Serchuk, professor of art history at Southern Connecticut State University (SCSU). Camille suggested that I contact SCSU adjunct professor of photography Stefan Znosko, who then put me in contact with one of his photography majors, Jessica Zielonka. Jess took the project on during her last semester at school, no mean feat considering that she was producing photos for this project at the same time she was putting together her senior exhibit. Jess brought in another SCSU student, Robert Velez, to round out our group, and together we three spent many productive mornings in the search for New Haven objects. In addition to the museum research visits and photography, a third area of support was also required, and again, I was fortunate. Claire Ammon is a professional genealogist, a rare find, especially among anyone younger than the World War II generation. Claire tracked down newspaper articles for all of the celebrations I requested, especially helpful since I was in the middle of moving to Virginia and had little time available for this important but time-consuming work.

Finally, thank you to my advisor at Salve Regina University, Charles Watkins, who is a great resource for American material culture and museum studies,

Photograph of Reverend Leonard Bacon.
*Courtesy of the Whitney Library, New Haven
Museum, Dana Scrapbook Collection, vol. 48, page 38.
Photograph by Jessica Zielonka.*

and to Ryan Finn, my copy editor at The History Press, once also a fellow student of Professor Watkins. Thanks to my dear friend Kellie Kiel for many years of tea, talk and after-school lunches at Celtica and Anna Liffey's. Last but not least, I thank my own "Three Judges" (or the "Three Jeffs"): Bristol, Connecticut born and bred Jeffrey Saraceno, my commissioning editor at The History Press, has been a pleasure to work with, as he was flexible, available and sensible with an understanding of the transition of northern life to southern; Jeff Karon, an independent editor with a sound grasp of the different ways in which to write; and, of course, Jeffrey Nichols, who took a big leap of faith this year that was not the easy path. His diligence, intelligence and good heart make him a very good museum director, and I am proud of him.

Leonard Bacon, one of New Haven's first historians and a pastor of Christ Church, wrote the following after finishing his *Thirteen Historical Discourses on the Completion of Two Hundred Years*, the book he was inspired to write after New Haven's second centennial celebrations in 1838. It was a pleasure to read the words with which he ended the preface to his first book. How right he was!

Had I been told twelve months ago, that within a year I should prepare and publish such a volume, gathering the materials from so many different sources, few of which at that time even explored, I should have smiled at the extravagance of the prediction. Yet the work has been done, and that in the midst of public labors and domestic cares. And now in dismissing the last page of a work which with all the fatigues and midnight vigils it has cost me, has been continually pleasant, I desire to record my thanks to the divine providence which has permitted me to begin and finish this humble memorial.

PART I
COLLECTING NEW HAVEN CELEBRATIONS

*Every passion borders on the chaotic, but the collector's passion
borders on the chaos of memories.*
— "Unpacking My Library," Walter Benjamin, 1931

Banners, ribbons and medals. Postcards, posters and photographs. Buildings, monuments and books. These are the cultural memory objects that remain from specially designed events marking milestones such as centennials and other anniversaries. The status of these types of objects ranks low on the measuring stick of museum collecting, and thus they are often marginalized in scholarship and exhibitions. Ribbons worn on the breast can't compete against bigger-ticket items such as furniture, paintings and the decorative arts, and because much of this was ephemeral in nature and designed and produced locally and for locals in large quantities, these objects are not afforded the same level of critical attention or assigned a high cultural value. However, when integrated into a story as this one—the way in which New Haven celebrated centennials and other significant milestones—their value as part of the whole is manifest.

In her groundbreaking 1988 book *George Washington Slept Here*, Karal Ann Marling assessed the impact of the American centennial in 1876 on popular culture in American society, stating that "centennial spreads the fever for collecting." This collecting was both of reproductions (such as the wooden nutmeg made from Charter Oak wood) and relics (anything associated to Washington would do). In New Haven, we can begin to comprehend some of the sentiment and the political/social agenda of such celebratory activities through a study of the traditions and the objects produced and collected. This effort—in combination with observing the special places situated at the heart of Elm City celebrations, contemporary news accounts of the events and, later, photography—helps us to grasp the meaning of these New Haven celebrations. Their frequency and size, especially in the second half of the nineteenth century, is proof enough of their importance, thus the question becomes not *were* these celebrations significant, but in what ways? And how did these celebrations contribute to shaping New Haven identity?

It is not only ephemera and mass-produced objects that come from marking special anniversaries—historic documentation and scholarship of lasting value has also been a byproduct of New Haven celebrations. For example, in 1831, five years after the jubilee (the fiftieth anniversary of the Declaration of Independence), John Warner Barber published his *History and Antiquities of New Haven, Conn.*, one of the first publications attempting to give an overview of Elm City history. Richard Hegel, New Haven's municipal historian who died in 2012, wrote that Barber's work was intended to address a burgeoning interest in locality but was also the beginnings of writing nationalist American history (earlier, American history had been written by Europeans).

With New Haven's so-called second centennial celebration in 1838, the writing of local history and the creation of an iconography central to New Haven identity were firmly established. From here, the dual commemorative form of book and medallion became a tradition that continued through to the end of the twentieth century, with the American bicentennial in 1976 producing the most material of all. With assistance from the New Haven Bicentennial Commission, Elizabeth Mills Brown published *New Haven: A Guide to Architecture and Urban Design*, which remains the go-to overview of architecture and city planning for the Elm City. In addition, in 1976, Rollin Osterweis published his book *The New Haven Green and the American Bicentennial*, and a separate portfolio of historic images of the city was published. More scholarship was undertaken in the form of a multiyear archaeological excavation at the Eli Whitney Armory site, supported by the bicentennial commission, about which a report was published in the *Journal of the New Haven Colony Historical Society* in 1977. The commission also supported the radio broadcast of fifty short history programs on WELI, while the New Haven Colony Historical Society published Christopher Collier's *Roger Sherman: Puritan Politician* in its Monograph Series. Finally, *New Haven Celebrates the Bicentennial*, a souvenir book covering the contributions of New Haven's many ethnicities, was also published—a result of the growing awareness of the ethnic heritage of the city that had been building from the tercentennial in 1938. The formal inclusion of ethnic heritage in the Elm City culminated in 1988, during the city's 350th birthday celebrations, from which the Ethnic Heritage Center was founded. New Haven 350 also saw the publication of Richard Hegel and Floyd Shumway's "New Haven: A Topographical History" in the spring 1988 edition of the *Journal of the New Haven Colony Historical Society*. New Haven was not the only entity to mark milestones, however. Yale's own identity was shaped by centennial celebrations. In 1901, the university erected its Bicentennial Buildings composed of Woolsey Hall, University Commons and the Memorial Rotunda on Hewitt Quadrangle.

The present book is the first publication to collect, as it were, New Haven's celebrations. It is not exhaustive—in addition to the milestone anniversaries written about here, there were many other events, hundreds quite probably, that occurred between 1781 and 1988 (the first and last events discussed), some of which continue today. These were military marches, drills and parades; victory parades for local political elections; holiday parades, including Columbus Day, St. Patrick's Day and Halloween; religious celebrations such as Three Kings Day and the processions and feast days of Roman Catholic churches; and special neighborhood events such as the Freddy Fixer Parade, first held in the Dixwell-Newhallville community in 1962. There were also special one-time celebrations on an immense scale, such as the Monument Day dedication celebration in New Haven on June 17, 1887; the Connecticut tercentennial celebration in 1935; and the many smaller events centered on the dedication of flagpoles, monuments and memorials.

However, due to limited space and time, my work is focused on the milestone celebrations that contributed in large part to shaping a particular New Haven identity, one based on episodes selected from a rich trove of people and events from history, as well as, equally, the exclusion and/or stereotyping of other people and events. It's not the whole enchilada—no one can write a full, inclusive history as there is too much that is missing for good. For example, how did food taste in New Haven in the eighteenth century? What did it sound like on Long Wharf when vessels docked and unloaded their goods? What was it like to ride in a New Haven built carriage? This book, however, demonstrates something of great value in that these celebrations were intrinsic to shaping New Haven identity in particular ways. Their reverberations echo today in New Haven memory—"the perpetuation," as George Kubler wrote, "of the original impulse."

SEVENTEENTH-CENTURY NEW HAVEN CELEBRATIONS

During the 1838 celebrations for New Haven's second centennial, the *Daily Herald* wrote that there were no celebrations held in 1738—despite the centennial of the founding of the New Haven Colony—because, the newspaper surmised, early New Haveners "were more urgently employed in the service of God, and the protection of their homes and families from the incursions of a savage foe, [thus] they had little time to devote to what then might have been considered idle pageant." In addition to characterizing Native Americans with the dual denigration of "savage" and "enemy" (despite the fact that the local Quinnipiacs were small in number and had agreeably signed treaties with the colony almost right away, placing themselves onto the first Native American reservation in the New World, on the East Shore), the *Daily Herald* missed one of the core reasons for the non-celebration of the centennial of the founding of the New Haven Colony. New Haven began as an independent colony in April 1638 and was eventually joined by other places within the New Haven Colony jurisdiction, including the neighboring towns of Milford, Guilford, Branford and, farther away, Stamford, Greenwich and Southold, Long Island. These first settlers, under the leadership of Reverend John Davenport and the entrepreneur Theophilus Eaton, quickly began to shape the town with their famous Nine Square Plan, which has been linked to both Christian theology and Judaic temple plans, a physical construction of the Old and New Testaments.

New Haven's stringent adherence to the Puritan worldview meant that most musical instruments were denied (except the jaw harp and the snare drum), as were celebrations such as Christmas. This, however, would not have precluded New Haven from engaging in communal celebrations such as days of prayer—also known as Thanksgiving. There were no newspapers available in Connecticut before 1755 when James Parker began the *Connecticut Gazette* in New Haven, and thus information about how the city might have marked 1738 with prayer or otherwise is unknown, but even the sesquicentennial of New Haven's founding fifty years later in 1788 was not marked in any special way. One reason for the lack of noted celebrations is that in 1665, less than thirty years after settlement on the plains of "Quinnipiack," the New Haven Colony was absorbed into the larger Connecticut Colony and remained part of this legal jurisdiction until the Declaration of Independence in 1776. Displeased with losing its independent status in 1665, it's likely that in 1738 New Haven did not honor its founding with any purposely developed sense of history or need for individual identity building. The desire—necessity even—to undertake this kind of memory work would really begin fifty years after the new country was birthed, with the special celebrations of the American jubilee.

The following chapters reveal that New Haven marked anniversaries of the city's Puritan establishment by inscribing tablets and other memorials and by creating works of public art depicting New Haven's genesis scene (such as Davenport preaching under the oak). Their lives and leadership were held up as models during anniversary celebrations until the late twentieth century, when an attitude shift occurred toward the Puritans. No longer invoked as role models, Puritans were trotted out only to establish historical flavor and not much more. It is interesting to note that while New Haven Puritan culture became the foundational theme on which New Haven would design its anniversary celebrations (always centered on service, with oration in Center Church), only the founding story was of interest to successive generations of New Haveners. Only at the tercentenary historical pageant were the Puritan New Haven stories of "The Loading of the Great Ship/The Phantom Ship" and "The Regicides" reenacted. Puritan New Haven was easily eclipsed by the city's Revolutionary War heroes and, later, by the city's industrialist leaders. Roger Sherman, Nathan Hale, the pre-treachery Benedict Arnold and Eli Whitney were more compelling figures than Davenport, Eaton and the Regicides, and they were closer in time and also closer in spirit to contemporary American life, whether of the nineteenth or twentieth century.

Treasures from Seveteenth-Century New Haven

Black clothes, buckled shoes and tall hats. Drafty houses and intolerant attitudes. Confusion over the difference between a Pilgrim and a Puritan. Supplicant Indians versus savage Indians. Old stereotypes of Puritan culture remain embedded in contemporary views, as hard to shake as any other long-held superstition or tradition. But if we surround ourselves with their things, can we uncover a fresh view? How about a bright red coat that belonged to a boy living in the colony? Or a chest carved by hand with fanciful geometric shapes and a tall cupboard inlaid with different colors of wood? What about the carved faces with fantastic fat wings that peer at us from gravestones in the crypt of Center Church? New Haven has some key works of material culture—that is, fine art, three-dimensional objects and documents—created by the Puritan transplants and their descendants. Beginning with the court records of the New Haven Colony—which denote the laws, the quarrels (one of the problems involved pillaging pigs) and the meetings of the early town settlement—we learn that laws were enacted, people were punished, Davenport tried unsuccessfully to start a college and the New Haven Colony saw little in the way of theft or other egregious behaviors, although apparently drunkenness was a problem from the beginning.

The New Haven Colony may have been an upstart endeavor (Davenport and Eaton, in fact, had not sought nor received a royal patent from the British Crown), with many people living roughly in simple timbered frame homes (the very first homes were actually half dug into the earth). But overall, the New Haven settlers were a wealthy group, and a description of Theophilus Eaton's home on Elm Street, directly facing the marketplace (or Green), gives us the sense that Puritans were not a dour bunch—if they could afford otherwise. In his new book, *Building a New Jerusalem: John Davenport, a Puritan in Three Worlds*, Francis J. Bremer described Eaton's house as "an E-shaped structure with five chimneys feeding as many as twenty-one fireplaces." The rooms were called by different colors—there was a green room named for the hangings (perhaps tapestries?) and a "blue room" used to store linen. According to Bremer, the "house and its furnishings were probably the grandest to be found anywhere in New England." The examples of the Puritan furniture you see here were made in New Haven, thus the patterns follow high-style European examples but were not as refined or as complicated in patterning.

Opposite: New Haven town record dated March 5, 1649, part of the New Haven City and County Documents Collections, 1648–1976. *Courtesy of the Whitney Library, New Haven Museum. Photograph by Jessica Zielonka.*

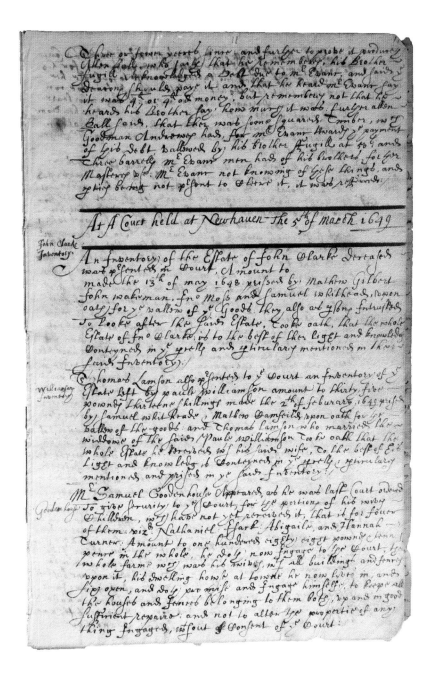

...... or fower yeere since, and further to probe it produce
Allen saith, who saith that he remembers his Brother
fugill acknowledged a debt due to mr Evanc, and said
Deacons should pay it, and that he heard mr Evanc say
it was £4 or 4li of money, but remembers not that he
heard his Brother say how much it was: further Allen
Ball said, that there was some squared timber, in ye
Goodman Androwes had, for mr Evanc towards ye payment
of his debt balanced by his brother ffugill at 50s and
three barrells mr Evanc men had of his brothers for ye
Mastery of sd: mr Evanc not knowing of these things, and
goeing being not present to cleere it, it was referred:

_____

At A Court held at Newhauen the 5th of March 1649

John Clarke
Inventory

An Inventory of the Estate of John Clarke deceased
was presented in Court, Amount to
made the 13th of may 1648 prised by Mathew Gilbert
John wakeman, fino Moss and Samuell withhead, were
oath for ye vallew of ye Goods, they also are ysome Entrusted
to looke after the saints Estate, tooke oath, that the whole
Estate of fino Clarke is to the best of their sight and knowledg
Contained in ye greatly and yt intirely mentioned in the
saint Inventory:

Thomas Lamson also presented to ye Court an Inventory of ye
Estate left by paule williamson amount to thirty five
powends thirteene shillings made the 2th of feburary 1649 prised
by Samuell whit Reade, Mathew Camsfield upon oath for ye
vallew of the goods: and Thomas Lamson who married the
widdowe of the said Paule williamson tooke oath that the
whole Estate he received wt his saint wife, to the best of his
sight and knowledg is Contained in ye greatly & yt intirely
mentioned and prised in ye saint Inventory:

Mr Samuell Goodenhouse Appeared, as he was last Court ordered
to give security to ye Court, for ye portions of his misery
Children, wt have not yet received it, that is for fower
of them, viz: Nathaniel, Elisab: Abigaile, and Hannah
Turner: Amount to one hundred eighty eight powend thenn
pence in the whole, he doth now Engage to ye Court ye
whole farme wch was his wiues, wt all buildings and fences
vpon it, his dwelling howse at towne he now liues in, and
shop, open, and doth promise and Engage himselfe, to keepe all
the howses and fences belonging to them both, vp and in good
sufficient repaire, and not to allow ye properties of any
thing Engaged, wthout ye Consent of ye Court:

Wainscot chair, red oak, maker unknown, 1650–80, gift of Mrs. Sarah E. Champton, 1973.3191. *Courtesy of the New Haven Museum. Photograph by Jessica Zielonka.*

Opposite, top: Chest, red oak with pine top, maker unknown, 1640–80, 1973.318. *Courtesy of the New Haven Museum. Photograph by Jessica Zielonka.*

Opposite, bottom: Child's red coat, worsted wool, gold band around collar, gold thread, beige lining, circa 1700. Museum records suggest that this long coat was probably worn by a boy between the ages of one and a half to three. The fabric contains a repeated pattern of leaves or ferns surrounding two flowers. The interior printed lining of the coat would have been imported from Europe. The coat has a date range from the mid-seventeenth to the early eighteenth century and was passed down through the Tuttle family, members of the earliest group of Puritan immigrants. The bright red color—an indicator of wealth—lets us know that Puritan culture was not limited to somber colors (or cheerless lives). Our contemporary conception of childhood is more directly a descendant of Victorian attitudes and ideals, and this little coat, cut in a style that mimicked adult clothing, shows us another way of looking at childhood. *Courtesy of the New Haven Museum. Photograph by Jessica Zielonka.*

Reverend John Davenport (1597–1669/1670), "Davenport Limner," circa 1670, 69.2cm x 58.4cm, 1750.1. This portrait was one of the earliest fine arts objects acquired by Yale College before the 1831 infusion of art via John Trumbull, which instigated the creation of the Yale University Art Gallery in 1832. Curator Susan Matheson wrote that this portrait of John Davenport, donated to Yale in 1750, "embodies the fundamental link between Yale College and the Congregational Church"—and to New Haven itself. This painting became the source for Davenport imagery down the centuries, replicated in engravings and modern works of art, including a U.S. Treasury Department–sponsored mural in the Westville Post Office painted in 1938–39. *Courtesy of the Yale University Art Gallery.*

PART II

EIGHTEENTH-CENTURY NEW HAVEN CELEBRATIONS AND REVERBERATIONS

When considering the first celebrations that New Haveners would have created, it is likely that special prayer services and orations were undertaken by Puritans at specific, regular times of year and also as special needs arose. In terms of New Haven's earliest secular celebrations, it is likely that the 1763 conclusion of the French and Indian War (called the Seven Years' War in Europe) presented New Haven with such a moment. New Haven participated in this war, its soldiers serving in the Connecticut militia, with one merchant turned soldier, Colonel Nathan Whiting, gaining accolades for his service at the Battle of Lake George. It is not hard to imagine that New Haven would have celebrated the return of its citizen soldiers after the Treaty of Paris was signed on February 10, 1763. Whiting died in 1771 and was buried at Grove Street Cemetery, thus missing out on the event that would commence New Haven's celebration culture: the Fourth of July.

Today, Fourth of July celebrations commonly feature reproductions of the Declaration of Independence, with its bold heading, "In CONGRESS, July 4, 1776," accompanied by iconic flourishes of fifty-six signatures at the very bottom. Using the document as a visual aid to celebrate the event, however, could not have taken place in 1776—the words of the Declaration of Independence could only travel as fast as men on horseback. So the questions arise: when did New Haven learn of the signing of the Declaration of Independence, and what did its celebration look like?

After the Continental Congress (including New Haven's Roger Sherman) adopted the document in Philadelphia on July 4, the *Connecticut Journal* reported six days later on July 10 that "[t]omorrow will be ready for sale, The Resolves of the Congress, declaring the United Colonies, FREE and INDEPENDENT states." One week later, the *Journal* went on to report that in New York City the "Equestrian Statue of King George III, erected in 1770, was thrown from its Pedestal and broken in pieces; and we hear the Lead wherewith this monument was made, is to be run into Bulletts." Comparatively, New Haven had no such monuments to the British empire, and nothing was said about crowds, riots or unusual happenings at the time. (There is, though, a portrait of King George I at Yale—the very first painting ever donated to the school by Elihu Yale himself; it is not known if the portrait was hidden for safekeeping.)

One week later, in the July 17, 1776 edition of the *Connecticut Journal*, the Declaration of Independence was printed in full. Again, no celebrations are mentioned anywhere, including New York, Philadelphia or Boston. The business—and busyness—of the war effort was paramount, including dealing with "enemies" who were Loyalists to the British Crown. In this same July 17, 1776 paper, there are numerous passages alluding to this new problem, including mention of a "number of enemies of freedom…and their Ringleaders taken prisoner." Thus, celebrating only began in the United States upon the successful conclusion of its first war, a date that continued to grow in scale and meaning both locally and nationally, reaching its peak with the American bicentennial celebrations in 1976.

Out of New Haven's experiences in the Revolutionary War, soldiers and their stories became key moments to celebrate over the course of the next two centuries. One could say, though, that New Haven's Revolutionary War stories are a bit *unusual*—New Haven, was, after all, the home of Benedict Arnold, reviled for supplying the British with local knowledge that helped their attacks along the Connecticut coastline but later celebrated for his leadership role on Powder House Day. Further, the day the British invaded New Haven was actually celebrated, rechristened to become the "evacuation" of the British despite knowledge to the contrary. Finally, in New Haven there are monuments to Nathan Hale, the Yale graduate/teacher turned Continental spy, but there is also, curiously, a British soldier's memorial in West Haven. These juxtapositions do more than just hint at the purposeful construction of history; they begin to illuminate the forces at play and the motives for writing history. In this part and again in the parts on the nineteenth and twentieth centuries, we will look at the ways in which New Haven celebrated the Revolutionary War, repeatedly rewriting the relationship between city and history.

PEACE CELEBRATIONS:
AMERICAN REVOLUTION, 1781 AND 1783

The most important, grand, and ever memorable event.
–Connecticut Journal, *May 1, 1783*

The successful conclusion of the end of the American Revolution provided New Haven with the fodder for celebrating, though the scale of the events was not as grand as what would come in the nineteenth century, and certainly not the bloated affairs of the twentieth century. When Cornwallis surrendered at Yorktown, the November 8, 1781 edition of the *Connecticut Journal* reported that "there has been great public rejoicing in this and neighboring towns." A group of New Haveners convened at the brick meetinghouse, where one of the Yale "tutors" (professor) gave an oration and a hymn was sung by students, and later, everyone dined at the statehouse. The *Journal* went on to note that "in the evening, the State House, College and all the Houses round the Market Place [the Green] were beautifully illuminated. The whole was conducted with the greatest regularity, good-nature, festivity and joy." The *Journal* then conveyed the news that the thirteenth day of December was to be marked by Congress as "religiously observed as a day of Thanksgiving and prayer throughout the United States." Whether this communal day of prayer actually occurred in New Haven is not known, as it is not mentioned in the *Journal* in either the December 12 or the December 20 edition. According to architectural historian John B. Kirby Jr., this first celebration was spontaneous, but by the time the Treaty of Paris was signed two years later, New Haven had plans for a much grander event.

The "public rejoicing for peace" was held on April 24, 1783 (not related, coincidentally, to either of New Haven's significant April dates: the city's founding date of April 25, which was not codified until 1838, and Powder House Day, whose anniversary, April 21, 1775, was not celebrated until 1905). The May 1, 1783 edition of the *Connecticut Journal* reported, "Thursday last was observed as a day of felicity and rejoicing in this town, on receipt of indubitable testimony of the most important, grand, and ever memorable event—the Total Cessation of Hostilities between Great Britain and the United States, and the Full Acknowledgement of their Sovereignty and Independence." This celebration provided the model on which New Haven would build its increasingly larger and more frequent celebrations. According to the *Journal*, the day began with the "discharge of thirteen

New Haven Treaty of Paris peace flag. Ezra Stiles, the president of Yale College and a leader of New Haven cultural life, drew an abbreviated sketch of a flag he saw on display during the peace celebrations in New Haven on April 24, 1783. Architectural historian John B. Kirby Jr. traced the design of the flag to a "tradition," from which Mrs. Roger Sherman and the widow of General David Wooster designed the flag themselves, erroneously using arms from Pennsylvania that they saw on the frontispiece from Roger Sherman's copy of the Holy Bible (today at the Beinecke Rare Book & Manuscript Library). The women had not realized that a national flag had been adopted in 1782. Though the flag no longer exists, this reproduction was made by needlework artist Jane Nettleton in 1983 from Ezra Stiles's sketch and description. The flag was the centerpiece for a joint symposium on the Treaty of Paris held by Yale University and the New Haven Colony Historical Society. *Courtesy of Jane Nettleton.*

cannon, paraded on the Green for that purpose, under elegant silk colors, with the coat of Arms of the United States, most ingeniously represented thereon, which was generously contributed upon the occasion by the ladies of the town." At 9:00 a.m., there was a service in the brick meetinghouse (which was reported as being crowded) and an anthem, while a prayer and thanksgiving were given by Reverend Dr. Stiles, president of Yale College, with an oration by Mr. Elizur Goodrich, one of the Yale College tutors. Another anthem was sung at the end. Afterward, a number of "respectable gentlemen of the town" dined together at the Coffee-House, and thirteen toasts were drunk:

> *To the United States of America, to Congress, to his Most Christian Majesty, to the United Province, to "Our Allies in Europe," to General*

Seal of the City of New Haven, silver seal mounted on brass base, 1.5" diameter. Made for the city upon its incorporation in 1784, the seal (seen here with its red wax impression) was designed by a trio of New Haven's post-Revolutionary leaders: Ezra Stiles, president of Yale College; James Hillhouse, war hero/politician/civic leader; and Joseph Meigs, a silversmith. Without the use of bold, graphic imagery, it's difficult to grasp the design: there is tall-masted ship sailing into New Haven Harbor, and the Three Churches on the Green are shown grouped tightly together at the top. There is also a classical pillar with twisting grapevines on the left. This seal design was not accepted, though the seal eventually adopted by New Haven in the nineteenth century and still in use today similarly features a ship, the sea and an inscription around the perimeter. *Courtesy of the New Haven Museum. Photograph by Jessica Zielonka.*

> *Washington, to the Confederate Army, to General Greene, to the Governor and the State of Connecticut, to General Warren, to the Permanency of the Union, to Universal, unembarrassed and prosper Trade with all the World, and finally, to "a cordial, sincere, and perpetual reconciliation with all our enemies, national and personal, internal and external."*

In the afternoon, cannons continued to be discharged at three, four, five and six o'clock "without any unfortunate accident." Foreshadowing many Fourth of July occasions to come in New Haven, fireworks were set off (including "rockets" and "serpents"). The finale was a bonfire on the Green at 9:00 p.m. Apparently, New Haven's celebration went well, whereas Hartford managed to set its statehouse on fire, burning it to the ground.

After the end of wartime and its peace celebrations, life in New Haven was reshaped yet again the following year. In 1784, many American cities were incorporated, including five in Connecticut: New Haven, New London, Hartford, Middletown and Norwich. New Haven's charter was granted on January 21, and the corporate name of the city was given as "the Mayor, the Aldermen, Common Council and Freemen of the City of New Haven." (The extended areas of East Haven, North Haven, Hamden and

Woodbridge were incorporated as separate towns during this period, leaving more or less the present shape of New Haven). Then, in 1788, Connecticut adopted the federal Constitution, which Roger Sherman helped draft. Both the 1784 and 1788 events would be the focus of centennial celebrations in the next century.

THE MODEL SHIP *CONSTITUTION*

We trust that as long as the ancient relic is in any way presentable she will in all historical and national celebrations be given the right of the line.
—letter to the editor, New Haven Evening Register, *July 3, 1884*

This ship model was New Haven's most beloved celebratory object. Though today it sits quietly in a museum case, the ship had an active social life at the end of the eighteenth and throughout the nineteenth centuries, appearing in numerous New Haven celebrations as a symbol of the link between New Haven and the sea but also of the desire of people to bring out "ancient relics" and rekindle the telling of local legends and national history. American cities had little in the way of historic objects as compared to Athens with its marble statuary, Rome with its ruins or Paris with its Catholic relics and the special containers (called reliquaries) that house them. Americans thus had to create their own versions of celebratory objects, imbuing them with memories and ideals (George Washington's set of false teeth falls into this category).

The story of this ship was reported in the *New Haven Register* on July 3, 1884, by a writer named T.R.T. Jr., who related that the model was picked up by a New Haven sailor near the mouth of the British Channel in 1768 on one of McAuley's vessels, and it was thus presented to the McAuley Firm on Long Wharf, where it was displayed until 1783, when the firm dissolved. From there, the ship went to Mix's Museum, where it again was on display until the museum closed in 1842. T.R.T. Jr. reported that a "Dr. Bennett" bought the ship at auction and upon his death in 1883 donated it to the New Haven Colony Historical Society. If the *Constitution* did indeed reside for much of its life at Mix's Museum, it must have been sprung loose regularly for special events. Not hard to believe, since these early "museums" were often more akin to entertainment complexes than quiet temples of the

Ship model, *Constitution*, circa 1750, gift of Joseph W. Bennett. *Courtesy of the New Haven Museum.*

muses; attitudes toward "using" museum objects were much different than our stringent "hands off" approach today.

The model ship pops up again and again when reading descriptions of New Haven celebrations. In the same letter to the *Register*, it was also reported by T.R.T. Jr. that this ship was carried in the 1783 peace procession in New Haven and was actually placed inside a captured British vessel drawn by American sailors during the procession. A later *Register* article from 1888 reported that the model ship was brought out again in 1784 for the celebration of New Haven's incorporation as a city and was carried in 1815 during the peace celebrations, in 1838 during the second centennial, in 1870 during the parade and in 1887 for Monument Day. No doubt the model ship was used many other times too. The *Constitution* was often seen at the head of parades, as reported in the July 5, 1888 edition of the *New Haven Register* ("the old relic attracted much attention"). The ship's importance as an object of memory is seen in the inscriptions painted onto the box stand on which it rests. On one horizontal side of the stand are painted the words, "Ship Constitution, found in the British Channel AD 1768, Carried in the Procession at New Haven, July 4, 1788, The Year of the Adoption of the Federal Constitution by this State." This inscription tells us how the model ship acquired its name.

The year 1788 produced a "memorable Fourth of July" in New Haven according to the *Connecticut Courant*. For labor historian Neil Hogan, the most significant aspect to this particular celebration was its participants, as he noted that "the spotlight was almost entirely on occupations and groups of workers." That is, instead of the sizeable contingencies of "veterans organizations, militia companies and military bands" one would expect in a Fourth of July parade taking place only five years after the end of the Revolution, the formal procession consisted of what might have been the largest ensemble of workers in any New Haven parade, even when compared to the late nineteenth-century celebrations, which often featured companies and their products. The list of participants provides a marvelous visual image, especially when one thinks of the assortment of men and their tools making their way from the "head of the long-wharf, through Fleet, State, Elm, York, Chappel, Church and Court Streets to the brick meeting house," with Elias Stillwell in the lead on horseback. It is worth the space to share them as printed in the *Courant*:

> *A plow drawn by ten oxen,*
> *Sowers,*
> *Reapers, with their sickles,*
> *Thrashers with their flails,*
> *Hay makers with their rakes and forks,*
> *Butchers, Barbers, Distillers, Bakers,*
> *Tanners, Curriers and Leather dressors,*
> *Cordwainers in a wagon on their benches at work,*

Sadlers, Chaisemakers & c. in a coach, making harnesses,
M [?], and Stone cutters with their trowels and chissels,
Cabinet makers, Joiners & c. with their various implements of mechanism,
Goldsmiths and jewelers with a silver Urn beautifully engraved and
spangled with ten stars emblematical of the ten states, which has adopted
the Constitution,
Coppersmiths and Braziers,
Watch and Clock makers,
Coopers with their adzes and broad axes,
Painters, Glaziers & c.
Hatters with their bows & c.
Weavers,
Taylors with their measures, shears, & c.
Suspended from a taylor's sign,
Boat builders, with their tools,
Rope-makers decorated with their hempen girdles,
Shipwrights, Mast-makers and Caulkers,
with their axes, rulers and adzes,
Black-smiths, with their bellows, anvil,
Hammers & c. in a wagon at work
In making hoes, one of which
They completed during
The march.
A Whale Boat with her crew
Captains of vessels,
Paper makers,
Printers, with compositing sticks galleys, and specimens
of printing displayed.
Merchants, citizens & c.
Schoolmasters followed by their scholars...
Physicians.
Tutors of Yale College.
Clergy of this and the neighboring towns.
City Sheriffs with the badge of
their office.
Common Council.
Mayor. Aldermen. Recorder.
Committee for the day, and Orator.
High Sheriff.

While Hogan pointed out that investigating the unusual arrangement of the procession, with the elites of society marching at the end instead of the beginning, would make a great study for sociologists and historians, as a material culture historian I am more interested in the second emphasis of the *Courant* story, which tells us how the ship model *Constitution* became a relic. After the procession went to services in the brick meetinghouse, there followed a dinner at the statehouse where the *Constitution*, which had already been part of the procession, "mounting twenty guns, as large as she could carry, under full sail, drawn by ten Seamen," was then displayed "directly over the table suspended…which had been prepared with a complete set of rigging." The *Courant* equated the finding of the model ship in the British Channel twenty years earlier to "the whole history of our Independence and glory in this miniature of naval strength."

At the dinner, the model ship was toasted and then later taken to the evening ball, "which was particularly ornamented with the company of the *Constitution*, whose beautiful appearance and expressive countenance engaged the attentions of ladies and gentlemen, and caused the greatest accord of federal feelings in both sexes." Thus, the model ship acquired its special status by providing a physical object to which New Haven could assign ideals about its newly formed republic. Almost one hundred years later, the ship was still an important part of New Haven celebrations, as evidenced by a second painted inscription on one of the short sides of the wooden platform, this one reading, "Carried in Monument Day Procession, June 17, 1887." Thus the ship model, a monument to the republic in New Haven, was eclipsed by the city's newly built Soldiers and Sailors Monument. By 1893, the *Constitution* was on display at the New Haven Colony Historical Society's new headquarters at 144 Grove Street, its days of active service over.

The Death of Adjutant William Campbell

No "storied urn or animated bust,"
No sculptured column stands to mark thy tomb;
No banner hangs above thy sleeping dust,
O Campbell! In the Abbey's sacred gloom.

Mourned by his comrades—honored by his foes—
"After life's fitful fever he sleeps well."
We raise this stone "his merits to disclose,"
His pity and humanity to tell.
—poem by Reverend A.N. Lewis, read at the Exercises of the Unveiling of
the Monument to Adjutant William Campbell, 1891

One New Haven Revolutionary War episode selected for commemoration was the death of British adjutant William Campbell. As a member of the invading July 5, 1779 British and Hessian armies, Campbell was killed in West Haven, but not before preventing the killing of local West Haven patriot-parson Noah Williston. During the invasion of New Haven (more about this larger event later, when it was renamed the "evacuation of New Haven" in 1879), hundreds of men were killed, and Williston was nearly killed himself by Tories in his own town when he was lying prostrate with a broken leg. The story goes that Campbell intervened with the words, "We make war on soldiers, not civilians," thus saving Williston's life. After getting a doctor to set Williston's leg and stopping the pillaging of West Haven homes, Campbell returned to the invasion effort and was shot by a sniper. He was carried into a house close by where he died. Here, the second part of the Campbell story commences, where history is continually rewritten (if not mythologized) through the rituals of commemoration and celebration. Though his grave lay unmarked for many decades, in 1831 John Warner Barber, New Haven's historian/antiquarian, placed a stone marked "Campbell 1779" close to the spot where he was shot, and in 1864, Campbell's dressing case, which had been purchased by John Townsend from Campbell's servant, was donated to the New Haven Colony Historical Society (the timing of the donation, during the Civil War, may not be coincidental).

Though the event took place in West Haven, and Campbell's grave site was somewhere in the vicinity of Allingtown, the New Haven Colony Historical Society owned the site from 1898 until 1977, when it was deeded to the West Haven Historical Society. The timing of the return donation was pressed by the West Haven Bicentennial Commission. By 1872, the stone marked with Campbell's name had gone missing—looting from grave sites is a practice that predates King Tut's tomb—and in 1891, a new stone was erected, thanks to the sponsorship of several Anglo-Scots clubs in New Haven. In the years that followed, Campbell's grave was again neglected (in 1976, the *New Haven Register* reported that the area was used as a dumping site), although seemingly his story was never forgotten. In 1949, a West

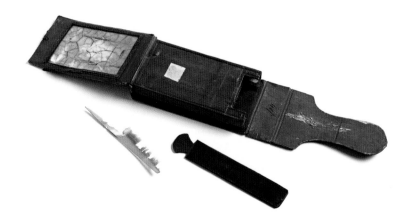

Dressing case belonging to Adjutant William Campbell, circa 1770s, gift of Lucius B. Townsend, 1865, *1998.403a-c*. This 5.5" x 3.5" leather-covered case (called "red morocco"), complete with comb and razor, was purchased by John Townsend from Campbell's body-servant, who had stayed in town to bury his master when he was killed in Allington (West Haven) on July 5, 1779. The case was passed down to Lucius Townsend, who donated the object to the New Haven Colony Historical Society. Other objects associated to Campbell were also noted in the memorial booklet dating from the dedication of his monument in 1891, including a handkerchief that covered Campbell's face (and perhaps was buried with him). His uniform was said to be worn by someone in about 1830 when the Milford Grenadiers marched on parade in New Haven. *Courtesy of the New Haven Museum.*

Haven schoolteacher named Marguerite M. Graham penned the following poem to Campbell:

> *He fell alas and broke his leg;*
> *Vainly for mercy did he beg,*
> *The soldiers would have run him through,*
> *Had Campbell but allowed them to.*
> *But truth 'twould have been hard to find*
> *A man of more humane mind.*

In 1976, the West Haven Bicentennial Commission seized on Campbell's story, and as the *New Haven Register* reported in the July 4 edition, "West Haven will be honoring the enemy." New Haven's Second Company Governor's Foot Guard reenacted Campbell's "humanitarian act and his later death atop Allingtown Hill at the hands of a sniper." The commission installed an iron fence around the monument to "keep out vandals," and the City of West Haven Parks and Recreation Department pledged to maintain the land, now designated as a small park. In the same *Register* article, it was also reported that the Pietro-Micca Club would install two flagpoles (one American and one British) at the grave site, though two flagpoles were also apparently in place on July 4, 1891, as during the dedication ceremony, it was noted that "the stone was veiled with the British and American ensigns, which were hoisted side by side and saluted."

There are very few commemorated burials of British soldiers on American soil, and this might explain the fascination that Campbell's story held for Queen Victoria in the late nineteenth century. In a series of correspondence reprinted in the memorial booklet produced for the Exercises at the Unveiling of the Monument to Adjutant William Campbell, Julian Pauncefote, who worked at the War Office on Pall Mall "On Her Majesty's Service," stated that Victoria "deeply appreciates the generous sentiments which have prompted the citizens of New Haven, after the lapse of so many years, to offer this honorable tribute to his memory." It was hoped that this connection would be repeated in 1976 when Queen Elizabeth visited the United States to celebrate the American bicentennial. She did make a brief stop in New Haven on her way to Boston but apparently did not visit the memorial site.

The third incarnation of the Campbell story surfaced in 2001, when the West Haven Historical Society rededicated the small park around the monument, with several companies reenacting the events, including the King's Rangers and the Second Company Governor's Foot Guard. But in an unexpected turn, the historical society announced in 2010 that it planned to sell the parkland and move the Campbell monument; this was reported in the July 19, 2010 edition of the *New Haven Register* as being due to "financial concerns" (specifically, the payment of the mortgage of the society's headquarters in the historic Poli House, which the group had purchased for $425,000). The plan received a great deal of criticism from the public—mostly, according to the *Register,* from "local history enthusiasts"—and by September 18, it was announced that the sale of the land was canceled. The City of West Haven had been at the ready to pursue an injunction against the sale, as the deed from the New Haven Colony Historical Society in 1977 stated that the West Haven Historical Society was required to "use and maintain the parcel of land as the gravesite and monument to Adjutant William Campbell and that failure to do so would result in the title's transfer to the City of West Haven." The president of the historical society soon resigned, and Campbell's monument remained in place.

TREASURES FROM EIGHTEENTH-CENTURY NEW HAVEN

In order to think and write about history, artificial constructs are used to help organize, define and interpret ideas, whether conceptual or physical. Sometimes these constructs fall short. For example, we could bookend the eighteenth century in the following way: in 1701, Yale College moved from its first home in Saybrook to New Haven, and in 1798, Eli Whitney purchased land on the New Haven–Hamden line for his armory. Thus, events at the beginning and end of the eighteenth century imparted core identity forms onto New Haven (as a center for education and manufacturing, respectively). These developments had repercussions on New Haven, the state and beyond. But a strict chronology leaves us wanting more: what was it like to be a woman in eighteenth-century New Haven? Or a parson turned soldier? And what did it feel like to be Benedict Arnold, unwanted everywhere he went? (His first wife is buried in the crypt at Center Church.) Can we find the answers to these questions in historic objects or in the words these people left behind? What about people living in New Haven who couldn't read or write, and what about their missing material culture (scholars call this a "legacy of absence")? The objects selected here are beautiful, historic and valuable on many levels. But there is much more to ask of them. In looking at historic objects from the eighteenth century, can we find the answer to what seems an essential question: how did New Haveners think about themselves before, during and after the Revolution?

Opposite, bottom: Silver presentation bowl, Cornelius Kierstede (1674–1757), silver, 8.6" x 19.1" x 8.7", 1745, 1913.688. Kierstede was trained in New York in the "Holland Dutch" style but eventually moved his business to New Haven in the 1720s, where he had acquired mining rights for copper. He was New Haven's first resident silversmith; his house/workshop was on Church Street, where he worked on commission to wealthy Elm City families. This bowl, though, was given by the class of 1745 as a gift to Yale College tutor Thomas Darling when he retired. There is much to be read into the decorative design of this bowl according to the Yale University Art Gallery; the choice of a silversmith working in a dated style associated to New York was a statement in favor of a more inclusive religious attitude at the university as preached by Darling, a response to the ultraconservative administration of president/rector Thomas Clap. *Courtesy of the Yale University Art Gallery, bequest of Miss Helen S. Darling, in memory of Thomas Darling, BA 1836, MA 1839.*

Right: Woman's blue pocket. If you were an American woman in the eighteenth century, and your skirt didn't have pockets—which was the norm—you would certainly want a pretty pocket such as this to carry small items. In parallel, your house likely didn't have any closets either, so owning a blanket chest or cupboard was another opportunity to showcase your taste and wealth through material and decoration. The color blue comes from indigo, a word meaning "from India," which was actually the plant woad. Indigo dye was lightfast and fade-proof and thus a very valuable trading commodity for European governments, many of which cultivated the plant in the New World, including the English, who grew woad in the Carolinas. *Courtesy of the New Haven Museum. Photograph by Jessica Zielonka.*

Powder horn, maker unknown, owned and inscribed with the name of Jabez Turner (1756–1847), 1778, 1979.22. This powder horn features carvings of ships, animals eating plants and mermaids. *Courtesy of the New Haven Museum, gift of Catherine White Turner. Photograph by Jessica Zielonka.*

Pointed Ray Fugio cent, copper, 1787, designed by Benjamin Franklin, diesinker Abel Buel, 28.6mm, 2001.87.29384. Buel cut the dies for the Fugio cent at the New Haven Mint/Company for Coining Coppers, located on Water Street between the old Sargent Factory and the C. Cowles Company. The Fugio cent is also known as a "ringed copper" or a "Franklin Cent" after its designer, and it appears in slightly altered forms. Thousands were produced in New Haven—the Yale University Art Gallery has about two hundred examples of the Fugio. In total, 1.4 million coins were minted in New Haven before the company dissolved. The representations on the obverse of the coin include rays of the sun, the Latin word *fugio* and a sundial, together indicating that "time flies." The reverse depicts an interlocking chain, the thirteen rings representing the original colonies. *Courtesy of the Yale University Art Gallery, transfer from the Sterling Memorial Library, Yale University.*

PART III

EARLY NINETEENTH-CENTURY NEW HAVEN CELEBRATIONS

The first half of the nineteenth century commenced with the death of George Washington. The retired president died on December 14, 1799, and his passing prompted a ritual of public commemoration that touched nearly everyone at the turn of the nineteenth century (New Haven most likely first read about Washington's death in the December 26, 1799 issue of the *Connecticut Journal*). Though Washington was not a young man—he was considered a vigorous sixty-seven—he had caught a cold during a horseback ride in the rain while inspecting his plantation. But his swift death was unexpected, and this, together with the paternalistic role assigned to him by Americans (famously described by friend Henry "Light-Horse Harry" Lee as "first in the hearts of his countrymen") produced a palpable public response. The objects and materials that New Haven (and hundreds of other cities) produced after Washington's death demonstrate the depth of formal mourning. Public services for Washington were held in New Haven in the brick meetinghouse on February 22, 1800, but two days before, Reuben Moulthrop had put on display a wax tableaux of the "Death of Washington" at his Court Street waxworks. New Haveners were instructed to wear black ribbons, on the left arm for men and women, "in such manner as they deem proper." There were drawings, engravings printed on ceramics, needlepoints, and memorial poems, including Theodore Dwight's (brother of Yale College president Timothy) "Lines on the Death of Washington."

Though there are differences between commemorating death, war and the darkest of human suffering—such as the Holocaust and

America Lamenting Her Loss at the Tomb of Washington, Harriet Cutler, silk, metallic thread and watercolor on satin, circa 1800. *Courtesy of the New Haven Museum.*

transatlantic slavery—and celebrating anniversaries and jubilees, there is also commonality between the two. These communal cultural practices are designed to make public statements about history, identity, values and place. For example, Washington's death is just one of these many types of commemorations, which in New Haven became staggering in size and frequency—especially considering that these events were planned and managed by volunteers. By the end of the nineteenth century, bunting in New Haven must have been worn thin from the constant use. Washington did not live to see the return of his "adopted" son, the General Marquis de Lafayette, in 1824–25 (Lafayette did visit Mount Vernon to pay respects at Washington's tomb), but for Connecticut and the other twenty-four states that the Marquis visited on his triumphant two-year tour, parades, orations, dinners and toasts were given to the "Nation's Guest." As Andrew Burtstein recounted in his book *American Jubilee*, Lafayette had been invited by James Monroe, the last Revolutionary War veteran to serve as president, in anticipation of the fiftieth-anniversary jubilee.

Lafayette visited New Haven on August 21, 1824, en route to Boston. New Haven historian John Warner Barber described the event as commencing with bells, the discharge of twenty-four guns and illuminations all around the city. In addition, a large sign with the words "Welcome Lafayette" was displayed in front of Morse's Hotel on Church Street, accompanied by American and French flags. A procession led the Marquis to the Court of the Common Council, where he was formally greeted by the mayor and where he shook hands with "hundreds of the citizens as they were presented." Women and children from New Haven apparently got the second shift. After breakfast, according to Barber, "more than three hundred of whom [women], with their children, had the pleasure of a particular introduction to the General." In the end, Barber wrote, Lafayette, "pressing his hand on his breast...said he was delighted with the manner of his reception by every kind of person."

After the introductions, Lafayette proceeded to visit the troops displayed on the Green, including the Iron Greys and the Foot Guard, and then was taken by barouche (carriage) to Yale's campus, where he visited the Cabinet and library and then went on to visit the "new Burying Ground" (Grove Street Cemetery), where he viewed the grave of another of Washington's aides-de-camp, David Humphreys. His final stop was a visit to Professor Benjamin Silliman's house (his mother-in-law, Mrs. Harriet Trumbull, was widow of Governor Jonathan Trumbull Jr., who was Washington's secretary and aide-de-camp). Ten years later, New Haven again commemorated Lafayette when James Hillhouse gave a public oration in June 1834 upon the death of the Marquis. A gun salute on the New Haven Green was fired, and ships in the harbor were requested to raise their flags.

One other event in 1825 will be described briefly: the celebration surrounding the groundbreaking ceremony for the Farmington Canal (also called the New Haven and Northampton Canal). The Farmington Canal, a private civic project led by prominent New Haveners such as James Hillhouse, was intended to provide access from New Haven Harbor into the interior of the state of Connecticut, as well as north into Massachusetts and beyond. The groundbreaking ceremony was held in Granby (close to the Connecticut/ Massachusetts state line) on July 4, 1825. Attendees did not foresee that the canal, fully opened by 1835, would be eclipsed so quickly by the development of the steam locomotive.

The Farmington Canal celebrations were lighthearted. John Warner Barber reported that one man, Captain George Rowland, rigged a boat with wheels, an awning and an American flag and proceeded to drive up the towpath, eliciting "numerous exhibitions of grotesque wonderment, from the surprised staring residents on the road." The next year, with great optimism, Mr. George Blanchard attended New Haven's jubilee celebrations and gave a toast to "the Farmington Canal Celebrations—may its anniversary be hailed as only second to our National Independence." Of course, there would be no anniversary celebrations for the Farmington Canal, owing, some believed, to the bad omens that accompanied the celebrations in Granby. First, a ceremonial wooden spade was given to Governor Oliver Wolcott, who, according to Barber, "at the signal from the canal commissioners…broke ground, and—doubly nerved with zeal and energy—soon broke the spade." Another omen came in the form of the "spontaneous celebrations [that] broke out the day before," according to historian/artist Eric Sloane, who wrote that "the clergy who had gathered for the occasion led to the prophecies of doom because of the Sabbath-breaking."

Spade, wood and paint, maker unknown, painting of James Hillhouse by William Giles Munson, 1825, 1971.425. *Courtesy of the New Haven Museum. Photograph by Jessica Zielonka.*

Peace Celebrations: War of 1812

To Commerce—It drags *on wheels; may it soon* glide *under sail.*
—after dinner toast, Mr. Butler's Hotel, New Haven, July 4, 1814

While this chapter takes a close look at the two most important anniversary celebrations before 1850—the American jubilee in 1826 and the second centennial (bicentennial) of the city in 1838—there were many other celebrations, including numerous Fourth of July celebrations, though the level of these celebrations likely waxed and waned, as the June 27, 1814 issue of the *Connecticut Journal* reported, "[W]hilst the citizens of New-Haven are not deficient in public spirit, nor in those patriotic feelings which are inspired by a love of country, it is somewhat remarkable that, for several years, they have almost totally neglected the celebration of this great day of national glory." One week later, the newspaper followed up with the information that the Fourth of July was to be marked with services in the "White Haven Meeting House," with Reverend Dwight giving an address delivered by Senator David Daggett (called the "old cucumber orator"), who "took a concise view of the life and character of the European tyrant—marking the different stages of his progress, through the blood of the unhappy victims of his power to the throne of France and his final overthrow." The War of 1812 affected celebrating, "more generally than for many years, the anniversary of Independence," as the *Journal* reported. A "committee of arrangements" had planned for the bells to be rung at 11:00 a.m., with a dinner for one hundred guests at Butler's at 2:00 p.m. The drinking of "pertinent and enlivening toasts" was a standard feature of these celebrations, and they were published in the newspaper afterward.

The War of 1812 was a direct concern to New Haven due to the livelihood that many made from seaport trade and merchant-based commerce. In 1884, a letter writer to the *New Haven Evening Register*, using only his initials T.R.T. Jr., looked back at the War of 1812, highlighting the problems caused by the Embargo Act (called the "Dambargo"), including lost work for sailors. According to T.R.T. Jr., the sailors, hanging around the Elm City's port were idle and decided to put on a parade to protest:

In New Haven the procession was a long one. At its head rode a young man on a large white horse, carrying a black pennant with the word "O-Grab-Me"—an anagram of the word "embargo." Directly behind him were four American shipmasters—Eliakem Bontecou [he is noted in other articles as being the sailor who found the ship model], John Lumsden, Nathan Bradley, and Peter Storer, who carried the Constitution on their shoulders. The little ship had her colors drawn at half mast, and all the men in the procession wore black crepe on their left arms. The procession marched around the city and finally disbanded at the water pump on the green.

New Haven learned of the news of the signing of the Treaty of Ghent in the February 13, 1815 *Connecticut Journal*. The publishers of the *Journal* had gotten the news themselves from the February 12 morning edition of the *New York Commercial Advertiser*, with the full wording of the Treaty of Peace published by the Journal Office, New Haven, on February 20, 1815. New England towns all reported "universal gladness," with the ringing of bells, military orders on parade and, as the February 15 issue noted, "the forlorn ships at the wharves and docks, once more displayed their colors; and now the busy hum of the implements of the mechanic is heard on board many of them, in fitting them again for sea." The *Boston Gazette* also reported, "In New York, New-Haven, New-London and Providence, a general illumination has taken place." Reports from Providence, Philadelphia and Salem noted the same. New Haven apparently had a contingency, however small, of dissenters; the *Connecticut Journal* called them "some 'choice spirits' [who] could not find it in their hearts to rejoice at the downfall of the tyrant, assembled at the County Hall and celebrated the day in their own way."

But in another coincidence of timing, the signing of the Treaty of Ghent was announced with "the anniversary of the Birth of Washington" in 1815, "which Americans read with great joy." Though there was some dissension in the papers regarding the shape of the ceasefire ("if no commercial treaty has been concluded, what, in the name of common sense, has America been fighting for these years past? For what has she expended so much blood and treasure?"), the common feeling was one of relief and optimism. On February 21, the *Connecticut Herald* announced that a jubilee would be celebrated the next day, with proper attention paid to "prevent riot or disorder. It is hoped that New-Haven will not be an exception to the rule."

The February 28, 1815 edition of the *Connecticut Herald* described the celebrations as beginning at 11:00 a.m. at the "new brick meeting house" (Center Church had been rebuilt under the direction of architect Ithiel

Town in 1812–14), and at 1:00 p.m., there were gun salutes. At 2:00 p.m., a "large company of gentlemen sat down to a sumptuous public dinner, at Mr. Butler's Hotel. Dinners in the first style were also provided at Mrs. Babcock's, Mr. Buck's and Mr. Fowler's hotels." A few days later, on Wednesday evening, March 1, a ball was held "in commemoration of the return of Peace and Commerce" at the Assembly Room, which was reported as "delightfully and fancifully decorated with laurels, transparencies…and the flags of the different nations, among which, those of the U. States and G. Britain were most conspicuous. The company was very numerous and respectable."

Until 2008, New Haven was the home of a series of paintings considered to be some of the most valuable historic objects from the War of 1812. A series of four oil-on-canvas paintings had been commissioned by Captain Isaac Hull in order to record the events surrounding the defeat of the *Guerriere* by the *Constitution*, which earned its nickname "Old Ironsides" in the August 19, 1812 battle. An Elban-born artist living in Boston named Michele Felice Cornè took up this work, completing two series of four paintings (*The Engagement, In Action, Dropping Astern* and *She Fell in the Sea a Perfect Wreck*). In the *Connecticut Journal* on July 10, 1815, we see that one set

She Fell into the Sea a Perfect Wreck, Michele Felice Cornè, oil on canvas, 32.75" x 47.75", 1812, M27847.4. *Courtesy of the Peabody Essex Museum.*

(minus one painting) was in New Haven, as it was announced by Daniel Bishop that

> *Naval Victories, Painted by the celebrated Marine Painter Cornie, the Italian Artist. Three grand Panorama Views of the taking of the* GUERRIERE, *by the* CONSTITUTION *frigate, is just added to the* NEW MUSEUM OF FINE ARTS, *now re-established by the subscriber at his house in Church-street, three doors south of the Episcopal Church.*

Ironically, in 2008, the USS *Constitution* Museum in Charlestown acquired a derivative series of *Constitution* and *Guerriere* paintings done by George Ropes Jr., a student of Cornè's. Pleased with its purchase of the Ropes paintings, the museum proudly announced the news, stating in a press release that "Cornè painted the Guerriere series twice and these two sets reside in the collections of the U.S. Naval Academy Museum and the New Haven Colony Historical Society. These images in public collections will not be sold." Not surprisingly, the deaccessioning and sale of the *Guerriere* and *Constitution* paintings from the collection of the New Haven Museum in 2008 was a quiet affair, not appearing in any local news sources. Once a feature of the New Haven Museum's Maritime Galleries, today these four now belong to the Peabody Essex Museum in Salem, Massachusetts.

AMERICAN JUBILEE IN NEW HAVEN, JULY 1826

> *Peace to their ashes!*
> –Connecticut Herald, *on the deaths of Jefferson and Adams,*
> *July 4, 1826*

New Haven in 1826 was a small town centered on the Marketplace (or Green), with a bustling port and the dubious distinction of sharing co-capital status with Hartford. When reading the New Haven issue of the *Connecticut Herald* published on the Fourth of July, the impression given is that while marking the fiftieth anniversary of the Fourth of July (already codified in this way) was given its due, the mood was not all that animated. Or maybe it was just the rain. The newspaper began its desultory reportage of the event like so:

If either pleasure or profit is derived from our editorial lubrications, our readers this week will be deprived of benefit, and for the best of all reasons—we have truly nothing to say. Nothing has occurred among us, during the past week, worthy of particular note, unless it is the redundancy of frequent showers…no fires, no hurricanes…—no murders, no suicides and no failures—nor any thing "marvellous" from abroad, to command the elucidation of our editorial noodles, nor to fill the mouth of gaping wonder.

The writer then provided a brief overview of the jubilee procession, which was to begin at New Haven's Tontine Hotel, travel up Church Street to Elm and then to State Street and Chapel, finally arriving at Temple Street to listen to a reading of the Declaration of Independence and an oration. An invitation was offered to "strangers and visitors" to buy tickets to the event, but the writer wasted no more time on exhorting citizens to show up. Most of the page was devoted to the latest finance news, reports about deaths from starvation in England, negotiations between France and Haiti and Spanish Constitutionalists who were executed or in exile.

Fortunately, so to speak, both Thomas Jefferson and John Adams died that day, furnishing the journalist with a valuable lead for his follow-up story on the jubilee celebrations in New Haven, Milford, North Branford and even as far north as Waterbury and Oxford. Thus, one week later, the *Herald* published a long account of the deaths of the ex-presidents (Jefferson clearly won the lead with print space). The writer's romantic pen was unleashed:

It is just as every American, every admirer of these venerable patriots could have wished—that, having endured beyond the ordinary terms of mortality, oppressed with years, they should have descended together to the grave on that glorious and auspicious day when millions of hearts were swelling with gratitude and praise to the fathers of the republic, and glowing with aspirations to the throne of Grace for their temporal and eternal happiness. Peace to their ashes!

Continuing with the sentiment, the jubilee in New Haven was reported in the *Herald* as being "in a manner surpassing anything of the kind ever before witnessed in our city." The thick description of the daylong event means that though photography was not yet available (daguerreotypes were not invented until 1839), a visual picture of the celebrations can be summoned easily. As the heart of the Elm City was (and remains) the Green, the location for sacred and civic ceremonies from its Puritan establishment forward. By

Tontine Hotel, engraving by John Warner Barber, Dana Scrapbook Collection. *Courtesy of the Whitney Library, New Haven Museum.*

1826, much of what we still know about the Green was already in place, including the iconic Three Churches—all less than fifteen years old in 1826. Also of importance was the statehouse (though this was not yet Ithiel Town's version, as that wasn't built until 1837). The Tontine Hotel was here, too, newly built in 1824 and not yet finished, though it was already a site for civic activities and was the subject of rhymes: "In our young city it is to be seen, as almost finished a new Tontine."

A sunrise national salute was fired, and processions began, the first located at the Mechanics' Society Hall which proceeded to the statehouse. A second procession was formed in front of the Tontine Hotel, and the Declaration of Independence was read a second time; from here, the crowd went to North Church for more oration and blessings, after which everyone went back to the hotel. Not everyone, of course; without the voices of women, people of color and everyone else not part of the "400 gentlemen" mentioned in the newspaper account, it is not possible to know how different people celebrated the jubilee, although we can hope that there is a New Havener or two who jotted down the day's events in a diary. Afterward, the newspaper related that "the Company dispersed at an early hour to enjoy the domestic circle," indicating that many small celebrations happened at home. All we know from the *Herald* is that these four hundred men must have been quite drunk, since they listened to more than thirteen "regular" toasts—all of which were sung—while sitting down to their "sumptuous entertainment" in the Tontine.

As you might guess for a dinner party of four hundred men remembering the American Revolution, Washington, Lafayette and "the Congress of '76" got their due, though the Greek War for Independence was toast number ten ("May the Cross soon to Triumph over the Crescent"), reminding us of the close ties that early Americans felt with other countries struggling for independence. In New Haven, there is a visual reminder of this. The Yale University Art Gallery owns an example of the most famous statue of the nineteenth century, *The Greek Slave*. One of the orators of the New Haven jubilee expressed the common sentiment: "On the next anniversary of our National Independence find her free from the Shackles of Despair." *The Greek Slave*, carved by Hiram Powers in 1843–44, worked on two levels: first, the reference to the establishment of a democracy, but second, the reference to the abolitionist

The Greek Slave, Hiram Powers, marble, 1851 after an original of 1844, 65" x 21" x 18", base 20.5" x 26", 1962.43. *Courtesy of the Yale University Art Gallery, Olive Louise Dann Fund.*

movement, as a young female nude (one of the first in American art) is depicted on the auction block, wearing shackles. Though the statue dates from almost twenty years after the jubilee, Americans identified with the struggle for Greek independence over a long period of time.

One of the last orations expressed at the jubilee came from "a gentleman" and was aimed at the competition between Hartford and New Haven for supremacy (both cities had their respective statehouses). This problem of co-leadership became apparent in just a few years when Hartford won the battle to become the capital city of the state of Connecticut. Of the contest between the two Connecticut cities, this New Haven gentleman toasted to "a fair competition in the race of internal improvements and a successful result to the enterprise of both." Today, of course, these cities, which sit so close to each other on the two ends of Interstate 91 in Connecticut, have fully developed independent identities and little interest in competition.

THE NEW HAVEN SECOND CENTENNIAL, APRIL 1838

Their children now in worship meet,
With mingled joys and tears,
In recollecting blessings great,
For twice-told hundred years.

–*"Centennial Hymn,"* Columbian Register,
New-Haven, April 24, 1838

The next significant anniversary celebrated in New Haven was the city's second centennial, called the "Centennial Celebration" (the term "bicentennial" was not in use at the time). Though vestiges of the jubilee reappear in the 1838 anniversary—that event was only twelve years earlier—it is this celebration that constructs the core model that New Haven would follow for another 150 years forward through anniversaries small and large. It was, in fact, one of the defining moments in the writing of New Haven history. New Haven residents recognized that they were about to shape a landmark event, as the *Daily Herald* reported on April 26, 1838, "this is the first instance of such a celebration, and as such demands peculiar record."

What this record looks like is composed of several endeavors: the making of history by codifying dates (i.e., designating April 25 as New Haven's official "birthday"); organizing the procession with prayer, oration and hymns at sacred New Haven sites; and the design and production of materials called by scholars "commemorative devices" that served the celebration and lasted beyond their contemporary use, including medals, badges, publications and plaques. The importance that New Haven gave to this celebration is seen fifty years later in a *New Haven Evening Register* article published on March 28, 1888, on the eve of the city's 250th celebration. The article notes that "each member will wear a badge which will be patterned very largely after that of 1838." The iconography of New Haven—that is, the visual pictures and symbols

Commemorative ribbons, centennial 1838 and Founders' Day 1888. *Courtesy of the Whitney Library, New Haven Museum.*

that represent aspects of city history and lore—are established during this celebration in 1838.

The Centennial Celebration was planned by the City of New Haven and the Connecticut Academy of Arts and Sciences, a group formed in 1799 to discuss and disseminate knowledge. (The academy, the third-oldest learning society in the United States, is still based in New Haven and continues to publish.) The April 21 edition of the *Columbian Register* reported that, in fact, plans for the Centennial Celebration were first discussed at the December 1836 meeting of the academy and that by the January 1837 meeting,

Professor James Luce Kingsley of Yale College was appointed chairman of the committee (Kingsley was a scholar of history, Latin, Greek and Hebrew and also served as Yale's librarian). The centennial committee approached the city about event planning, and a joint committee was formed, with the city committing $300 toward the expenses of the celebration.

The selection of the date of April 25 was one of the first things worked out by the committee. Its rationale for choosing April 25 was explained after the centennial in the April 28, 1838 edition of the *Columbian Register*. The Puritan settlers had sailed from Boston, arriving in Quinnipiack (the name chosen for the New Haven Colony) on April 12, 13 or 14, 1638, but Kingsley and his group were not able to pinpoint the exact date, thus the committee turned to the first sermon given by Reverend John Davenport under the shade of a large oak tree, which had been traditionally located at the corner of George and College Streets. Though Kingsley wrote that the study of his committee did "not lead to infallible conclusion…the balance of probabilities clearly inclines to the 15th of April, 1638, as the 'first Sabbath' kept in this town by the original settlers." However, the committee's work was not yet done, as an adjustment to the modern calendar system back to the seventeenth century had to be made, which produced a ten-day difference. New Haven's official birthday, and thus the date of permanent European settlement in New Haven, was codified as April 25, 1638.

The Centennial Celebration had echoes of the jubilee, with national salutes fired at sunrise and sunset, accompanied by the ringing of bells. Sacred New Haven spots were again used as the focal points for the program, though the committee proposed that a "flag staff bearing an appropriate banner will be erected in George Street, where the oak stood, under which the first Sabbath was celebrated." The committee also proposed "a similar display will be made in Elm Street, to mark the place where Theophilus Eaton and John Davenport, the Moses and Aron of the New Haven Colony, has their dwellings on opposite sides of the street." The procession, as during the jubilee, started at the statehouse and wound its way around George, State, Elm and Temple Streets, ending at Center Church. In keeping with the focus of the founding of the New Haven Colony, the procession, which apparently included women, went to the designated oak tree at George Street, which had become the representative sacred spot for Eaton and his group of Puritan immigrants, much like Plymouth Rock on the shores of Massachusetts became *the* landing spot for the Pilgrims.

In addition to these markings both on the landscape and on people, this is also the first time (but not the last) that a commemorative medal was struck

New Haven's second centennial (bicentennial) medal, Hezekiah Auger, engraved by Charles Cushing Wright, silver, 1838, 56mm, 2001.87.26286. *Courtesy of the Yale University Art Gallery, transfer from the Sterling Memorial Library, Yale University.*

for a New Haven anniversary. Not mentioned by name in the *Columbian Register* article is New Haven artist Hezekiah Auger, chosen for the task due to his standing as the city's finest sculptor. His delicate watercolor designs for the medal are on display at the New Haven Museum, along with a medal produced in bronze, although silver medals were also minted (the Yale University Art Gallery owns at least ten medals, but it has catalogued its examples under the name of the engraver, Charles Cushing Wright). Auger's life story reflects the struggle of early American artists to acquire enough artistic training and the patronage needed to sustain a professional life in the visual arts. (The more famous Samuel F.B. Morse, Auger's mentor and fellow inventor-artist, endured similar challenges.) The centennial medal, described in the *Register* as offering an "exhibit to the eye some idea of the changes which two hundred years have wrought in Qunnipiack," constructs, perhaps for the first time, an iconography for downtown New Haven, a visual imprint that continues to be used to the present day.

On the obverse of the medal, the inscription begins, "Quinnipiack 1638, The Desert Shall Rejoice," which accompanies the depiction of Davenport preaching under the oak, with East Rock and a small group of Quinnipiac Indians to the left. The reverse continues the biblical inscription, "and blossom like the rose," with a more complex design that condenses adeptly the insertion of technology into the "native" landscape. The scene is divided into three registers (or levels). In the lower register is the continuing importance of New Haven's location on Long Island Sound and its relationship to maritime trade (with a wonderful mix of old and new: a large three-masted schooner in the center and a steam-powered paddle boat to the left). In the center of the medal, the façades of the Three Churches on the Green are fronted with the newest technology to reshape society—the Hartford & New Haven Railroad had been chartered only five years before. In the third layer are the buildings of Yale College, located on the upper Green. New Haven's famous elms are shown to be crowding the spaces between the buildings, including the statehouse, which sits perpendicular to the rest of the structures on the Green. In the end, the heart of New Haven has been transferred from physical space to representation and will never leave New Haven consciousness. In other words, by 1838, New Haven's most venerated landmarks had been established and, through the production of this medal, became part of the visual language of the city. The strength of the medal's design is demonstrated by the fact that the 1888, 1938 and 1988 anniversary celebrations all reused Auger's design in some form, illuminating the depth of attachment that the visual arts and the writing of history have on collective consciousness (and vice versa).

The *Columbian Register* ends its article with an exhortation. "We hope our citizens will join in the procession and exercises of the day, and offer their tribute of thanksgiving that we still retain the holy privilege for which our fathers abandoned the soil of their nativity." Meanwhile, over at the *Daily Herald*, complaints were the order of the day. Sounding irritable, the April 23, 1838 edition noted:

> *Great complaints have been prevalent through the city in regard to the arrangements for the Centennial Celebration. Almost everything, as yet, is at hap hazard, as far as the public is concerned, for though it has been announced that a Committee of Arrangements has been instituted, the names of that Committee have not been announced, and hence the gentlemen nominated to officiate on the occasion are utterly in the dark in regard to the manner of performing their appropriate duties, and are without reference in regard to the subject.*

Apparently, this tactic worked, because the next day's *Herald* reported the Order of Procession, the route and the Centennial Hymn, which was much shorter (and appropriately focused on prayer) in comparison to "The Birth of New-Haven" song published by William Goodwin three days later in the *Herald* (featured at the beginning of this book). Also described were the divisions between people—gender, military and Yale, specifically—as indicated by the arrangement of seating in Center Church, with the north gallery and the "slips on the floor next to the wall" reserved for women, the main seating reserved for people in the procession (all men) and the south gallery reserved for the military and Yale students. In order to give its own staff the ability to attend the next day's events, the *Daily Herald* announced that it would take the day off from publishing.

From reports in both the *Daily Herald* and the *Columbian Register* after the anniversary, "all the exercises of the day were highly appropriate and impressive." The weather cooperated perfectly, which was read as being heaven sent but was certainly fortunate since much of the communal worship was done outside, at a platform erected at the intersection of College and George Streets, with a large banner reading "Quinnipiack 1638" on one side and "New Haven 1838" on the other. Children were an important part of the outdoor activities; they were not invited into the Center Church service—probably a good idea considering that the "immense concourse of children, by an unseen and yet simultaneous impulse, united their infantile voices in three hearty cheers."

Today, we would count the children fortunate that they were not packed into the crowds at Center Church, as Professor Kingsley himself spoke for more than two hours. Even the *Daily Herald* wrote that "to attempt an analysis [of Kingsley's discourse] we have neither the time nor room." The orations ignited the attention of Center Church's pastor, Reverend Leonard Bacon, who later wrote that "it seemed proper for me to notice in the pulpit an occasion so interesting…and I undertook to prepare one or more discourses illustrative of our ecclesiastical history." With the assistance of Professor Kingsley, Bacon then went on to present sermons on subsequent Sunday evenings that would become the subject of his first book, *Thirteen Historical Discourses on the Completion of Two Hundred Years, from the Beginning of the First Church in New Haven*. It took Bacon one year to compile and publish his work, but its genesis occurred with the Centennial Celebration. According to historian Richard Hegel, it is the first New Haven history publication of note produced in the nineteenth century and reflects the "rapid growth of local historiography after 1815 partially as a reaction to the expansion of nationalism and also a reflection of the competition between different parts of the country." Of course, Hegel could have said "competition between Hartford and New Haven" as well.

The *Columbian Register* wrapped up its coverage of the Centennial Celebration with a tone of *momento mori*, stating that "the return of this anniversary will find all its late participants in the tomb; but if the solemnities and recollections of the occasion shall tend to keep alive the spirit of patriotism and love of New England's peculiar institutions, the festivities of its advent

THIRTEEN

HISTORICAL DISCOURSES,

ON THE COMPLETION OF

TWO HUNDRED YEARS, FROM THE BEGINNING

OF THE

FIRST CHURCH IN NEW HAVEN,

WITH AN APPENDIX.

BY LEONARD BACON,
PASTOR OF THE FIRST CHURCH IN NEW HAVEN.

"Ye temples, that to God
Rise where the fathers trod,
Guard well your trust,
The *truth* that made them free,
The *faith* that dar'd the sea,
Their cherish'd *purity*,
Their garner'd *dust.*"

NEW HAVEN:
PUBLISHED BY DURRIE & PECK.

NEW YORK:
GOULD, NEWMAN & SAXTON.

1839.

Thirteen Historical Discourses on the Completion of Two Hundred Years, from the Beginning of the First Church in New Haven, with an Appendix, Leonard Bacon, Durrie & Peck, Publishers, New Haven, 1839. *Courtesy of the Whitney Library, New Haven Museum. Photograph by Jessica Zielonka.*

will prove a permanent blessing." The newspaper had earlier mentioned the "spectacle of such a multitude of the rising generation participating in the festivities of an occasion at which even they can never be present again." However, he wrote too soon, as even if no one in this celebratory group would be around for the tercentennial in 1938, New Haven was on a trajectory of celebrating for the rest of the nineteenth century.

TREASURES FROM EARLY NINETEENTH-CENTURY NEW HAVEN

During the dedication of the Bunker Hill Monument in Charlestown, Massachusetts, in 1825, Congressman Daniel Webster said, "Let our age be the age of improvement." In the twenty-first century, after the modernist agenda to wipe out the past, the postmodern deconstruction of meaning and the embrace of uncertainty, we naturally want to find an alternative view—an un-Websterian perspective—from which to look at objects from this moment in time. But it is difficult, as even the naming of the city, as a "new haven," suggested that New Haven used as its primary narrative this very purpose. Thus, the objects selected here speak with a cohesive voice as a motivating force for development or, to use Webster's word, "improvement." Even as we rely on this idea, though, it is a concept that continues to mutate, its forms altering from internal and external forces. Even those who attempt a strict adherence to *not* evolving—as do some sects of the Amish for example—do not remain untouched. Earlier incarnations of "improvement" in New Haven included the Puritan design of the Nine Square Plan and the continuous design and redesign of Yale College, but during the "long nineteenth century," downtown New Haven was drastically transformed, from the planting of elms to the development of Grove Street Cemetery, from the building/rebuilding of the Three Churches on the Green to the creation of the Farmington Canal and, finally, in the beginning of the twentieth century, with plans for urban redevelopment in the style of the City Beautiful movement.

Of course, the "long nineteenth century" did not take just one shape, and even in a relatively small city like New Haven, you will see easily differences in intent, style and use of objects between the first half and the second half of the nineteenth century. However, there is something compelling about the long nineteenth century. As Laurel Thatcher Ulrich wrote in *The Age of Homespun*, "Nineteenth-century Americans understood that objects tell stories. They wrote their stories in speeches, memoirs, and poems, and on scraps of paper that they pinned, pasted, or sewed to the things they saved." They did this in tandem with their stalwart belief in improvement, thus the objects selected here were saved for their stories but also speak to the "age of improvement," whether destined for self, city or country.

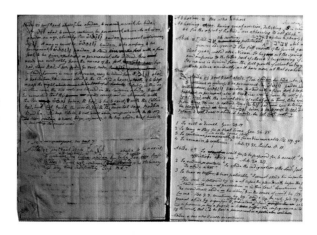

Notebook belonging to Noah Webster (1758–1843), notes for the letters "a" and "b" for preparation of the dictionary. In an endnote in the introductory chapter of his book *American Jubilee*, historian Andrew Burstein noted that the first edition of Noah Webster's *American Dictionary of the English Language* connected the word "jubilee" to its Jewish heritage (in which slaves were freed) with that of the Declaration of Independence, both of which speak to the idea of liberty. Webster graduated from Yale in 1778 and was later an alderman for New Haven. His widely and repeatedly published *Elementary Spelling Book* (known as the "Blue Backed Speller" due to the color of the binding) in 1783 provided the funds with which to write the first America dictionary, published in 1828. *Courtesy of the Whitney Library, New Haven Museum. Photograph by Jessica Zielonka.*

Opposite, top: Public lecture tickets, including lectures on "China and the Chinese" and a "Gentleman's Course Ticket." Founded in 1826, the Institute Library is one of the last membership libraries in the United States. The purpose of these early libraries was to encourage the "intellectual and moral improvement" of its members (in fact, its bookplate features the motto "Improve the Moment"). By 1835, the organization, which had begun as an educational resource for working men offering lectures, debates, a circulating library and classes, had opened its doors to women. New Haven historian and engraver John Warner Barber was an early librarian, but William A. Borden, the librarian at the end of the nineteenth century, created a unique cataloguing system still in use today. The speakers list from the nineteenth century is impressive—Ralph Waldo Emerson, Frederick Douglass and Henry Ward Beecher all lectured at the Institute Library. *Courtesy of the Institute Library. Photograph by Jessica Zielonka.*

Opposite, bottom: *A Collection of Plants of New Haven and Its Environs Arranged According to the Natural Orders of Jussieu*, Horatio Nelson Fenn, 1822, New Haven. Fenn was a Yale College medical student who collected almost seven hundred botanical specimens useful for practicing medicine. Later bound into four volumes, the Fenn collection is the earliest systematic study of plants in the state of Connecticut and is also one of the oldest in New England. *Courtesy of the Yale Peabody Museum of Natural History.*

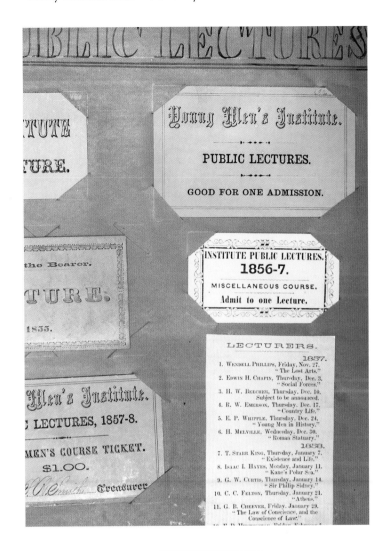

Buckskin coat belonging to Henry Eld, 2001.320. Eld's full dress navy uniform (hat, coat, epaulets and sword), this leather coat and a framed oil painting were given to the New Haven Museum by his daughter, Miss Eld, after her death in 1903. Most likely crafted by a Native American during Eld's travels in the Oregon territory, Eld wrote in his travel journal about meeting a man toward the end of his travels who refused to speak to him in English. "He looked up at my buckskin attire and scraggy beard that had not been shaved for fifty days and exclaimed, 'my God sir where did you come from?'" Eld died in 1850 on the voyage home to New Haven from Rio de Janeiro. *Courtesy of the New Haven Museum. Photograph by Jessica Zielonka.*

PART IV

LATE NINETEENTH-CENTURY NEW HAVEN CELEBRATIONS

Building on the patterns established during the first half of the nineteenth century, celebrations in New Haven reached a crescendo between 1865 and 1892 with no less than seven major events that attracted tens of thousands of spectators to the Elm City. These events included the end of the Civil War (and the mourning of the assassination of Abraham Lincoln) in 1865; the Fourth of July/centennial of the United States in 1876; the Fourth of July/centennial of the evacuation (or invasion) of New Haven in 1879; the Fourth of July/centennial of the incorporation of the city of New Haven in 1884; the dedication of the *Soldiers and Sailors Monument* in 1887; the Founders' Day/250th anniversary of the founding of New Haven in 1888; and the 400th anniversary of Columbus and the discovery of America in 1892. Interspersed with these major celebrations were smaller events such as military parades, ethnic celebrations and the usual holiday traditions that by the second half of the nineteenth century included a formal Thanksgiving celebration (given federal status by Abraham Lincoln in 1863) and a growing practice of celebrating Christmas with trees decorated with lights and ornaments.

Queen Victoria, the leading style maker of the era, married Prince Albert of Germany, and his national Christmas traditions permeated English culture, eventually subsumed into American life. The proliferation of factory-produced consumer goods created, as historian David Jaffee wrote in *A New Nation of Goods*, a "new culture of domestic consumption" on both sides of the Atlantic that embraced opportunities to display taste, style and a devotion to the ideals of faith, family and country, all of which Victoria and Albert embodied. But New Haven had its own Albert, according to the exhibit publication *An Ethnic History of New Haven*. A German immigrant and florist named Frederick Rehbein wove garlands of pine and laurel leaves into Christmas wreaths, which were popular with everyone in New Haven, German-American or not.

The United States had little time to celebrate the end of the Civil War before the assassination of Abraham Lincoln. By the first months of 1865, the end of the war was in sight, and Lincoln gave his second inaugural speech on March 4, 1865, a day that was spoken of in newspapers as a potential new "Republican holiday," demonstrating the prevalent Northern attitude of affection held toward the president (a sentiment called "Lincolnism"). On April 9, Confederate general Robert E. Lee formally surrendered to Union general Ulysses S. Grant at Appomattox, and the following week, the April 15, 1865 issue of the *Columbian Register* reported:

> *The news of the surrender of Gen. Lee was received with demonstrations of rejoicing in every city and village where the telegraph conveyed the intelligence. About midnight our citizens were aroused by the ringing of all bells in the city, the firing of artillery, and the blazing of bonfires. People leaped from their beds, with the joyful cry of "Peace!" on their lips, and hurried to the principal streets where all was hilarity and rejoicing over the news of Lee's surrender. The whole town was soon aglow. Chapel Street was a scene of general illumination—and in a short time everything combustible that would be got hold of, was blazing in the bonfires at the street corners.*

Apparently, the *Register* had not yet received the news that the night before, on April 14, Lincoln was assassinated by John Wilkes Booth. The celebrations turned to "intense grief manifested everywhere," and soon commemoration of "the National Calamity" began with the ringing of bells, flags being set at half-mast and homes draped in black fabric. On that Saturday, April 15, New Haveners learned of the event, and at 11:00 a.m., a notice was posted on the Green saying that a meeting would be held at the statehouse at noon. At this meeting, a "large and grief stricken congregation of men and women gathered at the south end of the State House," where Mayor Tyler presided, and Reverend Leonard Bacon offered a short prayer for "Divine Providence" and a resolution expressing grief and "our trust in Almighty God, the Rule of Nations as of the World, hoping and believing that He will overrule this dreadful event, to the good of the smitten people of our land and of our race." On Sunday, sermons and orations were given at churches, with pulpits draped in black fabric, and a national day of fasting was proposed. Following the nation's mourning period, New Haven's Fourth of July in 1865 was dedicated to the "Restoration of Peace." A sum of $500 was granted by the city, and a committee of arrangements put together a daylong event with races at Hamilton Park, steamboat excursions and fireworks.

Unlike the Revolutionary War, which reverberated through many generations of celebrations in New Haven through the veneration of Sherman, Hale, Wooster and even Arnold, the Civil War was instead about memorializing

Monument Day ribbon for the New Haven Fire Department, 1887. *Courtesy of Joseph Taylor.*

the dead through monument building; post–Civil War America was the country's first monument boom. This is underscored by the fact that only one Civil War story is used in any New Haven celebration: "The Death of Theodore Winthrop," was performed during Yale's 1916 pageant. This story recounts the first Northern death in the Civil War—when Confederate troops turned over the body of Winthrop, a Yale student, with full honors.

New Haven reconstructed its memory of the Civil War by erecting the 110' tall Soldiers and Sailors Monument, on the summit of East Rock Park in 1887. Many other Civil War monuments in New Haven continued to be erected right through until 1915, including the Admiral Foote Memorial (1863), the Knight Hospital Monument (1870), the Monument to the Ninth Regiment (1903), the Memorial to Connecticut Civil War Soldiers (Broadway, 1905), the Cornelius Scranton Bushnell Memorial (1906) and the Civil War Soldiers Memorial (1915). In 2008, these were joined by the Connecticut Twenty-ninth Colored Infantry Memorial. New Haven threw itself into the dedication celebration for the Soldiers and Sailors Monument, called Monument Day, June 17, 1887, amassing the largest crowds in state history. The "ceremonies were an unprecedented and perhaps never-equaled outpouring of civic pride and celebration," according to David Ransom. In numbers difficult to fathom today, 150,000 people watched while 20,000 people marched with revered guests William Tecumseh Sherman and Philip Henry Sheridan. Monument Day left such an impression on the city that a Centennial Celebration was held on September 20, 1987.

AMERICAN CENTENNIAL, JULY 1876

At 2 o'clock p.m. a grand BALLOON ASCENSION *will take place from the Public Square. The celebrated Aeronaut, Prof. Fisher having been engaged to undertake a "flight among the clouds" in his beautiful aerial ship the "Eagle."*

—advertisement for the Centennial Celebration, Columbian Weekly Review, *July 1, 1876*

The development and subsequent changes in the United States and in cities such as New Haven between the first half of the nineteenth century and the second half are appreciated when viewing the Elm City's celebrations for the American centennial in 1876 as compared to the 1826 and 1838 events. These changes can be expressed through population size—the United States was 12 million strong in twenty-four states in 1826, but by 1876, there were 40 million Americans in thirty-seven states—but it is of interest to discern how this growth in size and demographics and the accompanying shifts in economics and social/political outlook due to industrialization changed the nature of celebrations in the Elm City. Ground zero for the American centennial was Philadelphia, with each state and territory participating in events at the Centennial Exposition—the first World's Fair in the United States—but cities across the country such as New Haven held their own local events as well.

In fact, New Haven was instrumental in supporting Philadelphia and the country's first centennial; between June 10 and July 2, 1875, New Haven held a Centennial Exhibition of Antiquarian and Revolutionary Relics to raise funds to send to Philadelphia. This was a female-driven affair: the committee consisted of fifteen women and two men, with Mrs. Worthington Hooker as president and a Miss Davenport as treasurer. The display consisted of familiar historic objects, with the *Portrait of Roger Sherman* (owned at the time by Mrs. Martha Sherman White, now part of the Yale University Art Gallery) listed as object no. 1. More objects came from Eli Whitney, Benjamin Silliman, Mrs. Henry Peck, Reverend Joseph Brewster, Mrs. William Atwater, the Yale

Connecticut State Building at the Centennial Exposition in Philadelphia, 1876, possibly designed by Donald Grant Mitchell, an author and landscape architect. Centennial Photographic Company, Philadelphia. *Courtesy of the Whitney Library, New Haven Museum.*

College Library, the Trowbridge and Ingersoll families and Mrs. J.D. Dana. Some of the other "relics" on display included a teacup and saucer that once belonged to Aaron Burr; the Benedict Arnold shop sign and William Campbell's dressing case, both of which were on loan from the New Haven Colony Historical Society; and an assortment of Washington relics such as a dried lemon from a tree planted by him and a piece of his coffin.

In addition to the Connecticut State Building, Connecticut's presence in Philadelphia is highlighted in Machinery Hall, one of the specially built structures for the exposition. World's Fairs were first established by Prince Albert in 1851 at the trendsetting Great Exhibition of the Works of Industry of all Nations, or colloquially, the Crystal Palace (a nickname for Joseph Paxton's iron and glass structure). The purpose, as envisioned by Albert, was to display works of art and mechanical inventions in appealing demonstrations of national pride and showmanship. In Philadelphia, these concerns were at the state level, and Machinery Hall was of great interest to visitors, not the least because the titans of industry were often the men who planned these events in the first place (women's work was relegated to special "women's buildings," and people of color were marginally represented and not allowed to work on the event at all). A "special correspondent" to New Haven's *Columbian Weekly Register* traveled to the Centennial Exposition—one of the 10 million Americans who visited—and reported on what he saw, as well as the inconsistencies presented in the official exhibit catalogue. New Haven was represented in Machinery Hall, the special correspondent noted, in the "combined and independent boilers from H.B. Bigelow" (Bigelow would become mayor of New Haven two years later) and in other ways:

> *An extensive exhibit, not discovered in the catalogue…was that of the Peck Brothers & Co., of New Haven, who have a black walnut case, a portion of which is upright, giving them a large surface on which to display their wares, which are arranged artistically, and consists of brass and silver-plated cocks, nozzles, spigots and other articles that we might mention if we knew the names of them.*

The machines and objects of the New Haven companies were displayed alongside other well-known entities of Connecticut industry, including Colt Patent Manufacturing Firearms from Hartford, silk manufacturing tools from Holland Manufacturing Company of Willimantic, the Thames River Woosted Company of Norwich and Howe Sewing Machine Company of Bridgeport. The Hartford Steam Boiler and Insurance Company also

Boiler, Bigelow Company. *Courtesy of the Whitney Library, New Haven Museum. Photograph by Jessica Zielonka.*

displayed objects in Machinery Hall, exhibiting exploded boilers and "specimens of defective iron."

In New Haven itself, the Fourth of July Centennial Celebration first gets print time in the *Columbian Weekly Register* on July 1. Spread throughout that 1876 edition of the paper are different notices about the upcoming Fourth of July celebrations in New Haven and surrounding towns, ranging from the droll ("we cannot afford in these hard times to burn up a city," in regard to fireworks) to the downright critical ("from the appearance of our town, no one would suspect the centennial of the Declaration of Independence was in a hundred miles of Wallingford. About the only way patriotism exhibits itself is by lying in the shade and killing potato bugs").

The American centennial celebration in New Haven reused some elements of the 1826 and 1838 celebrations, but on the whole, it was a much different event, closer in presentation to twentieth-century celebrations. These differences include the less sacred tone of the celebration, the fact that the event had much less focus on New Haven's role in the American Revolution

(Roger Sherman and David Wooster, reverentially invoked during the jubilee, are marginalized) and the exponential explosion of secular activities that went after bright lights and profane performance. The whole purpose of the day was directed to the evening fireworks display, thus giving New Haven the regional role it continues to have right through to today as the place to watch Fourth of July fireworks. Malley's took out numerous ads for its "grand opening of fireworks," offering "a huge selection of fireworks and 'novelties,'" including torpedoes, Roman candles, serpents, long stick rockets and something called Greek Fire. In 1876, New Haven was setting itself up as the place to see "the grandest and most magnificent display of fireworks ever exhibited in New England" (although one has to wonder what Boston did for the American centennial and what it said about its own celebration).

The celebration was packed with more activities than anything seen previously. Though the day began much like the jubilee and the second centennial celebrations, with thirteen-gun salutes at sunrise and the chiming of bells, the end result was very different. After the early morning salutes and flag raising, the military company men said a few words, ate baked beans and hardtack and drank coffee, and "then the old camp fires were revived, old songs were sung and stories and speeches were made." According to the *Register* on July 1, a procession was formed of professional military units, including the Second Regiment Connecticut National Guard and the Second Company Governor's Foot Guard. Strangely, Yale students are not named a formal part of the procession (perhaps a symptom of surfacing town/gown problems). The *Register* commented that the decorations were "general—almost universal" (how much variation can you have with bunting?), but the whole city was thoroughly dressed.

The procession started out of the north gate on the Green, traveled up Elm to York, then went to Chapel, Wooster Place, Green Street, Olive, Grand, State, George, Church and, finally, to Elm and back to the Green. In this procession, the rapid growth of the city's fire and police services appear for the first time in an anniversary parade, as ten different steam engine companies participated. Also of note is the first appearance of Irish Roman Catholics in an Elm City anniversary (though Irish Americans in New Haven had been holding their own St. Patrick's Day parades since 1842). Four Roman Catholic societies, as well as their respective "temperance cadets," participated in the procession. The first Irish Roman Catholic church had been built forty-four years earlier at the intersection of York and Davenport Streets (recently the scene of an archaeological investigation due to the discovery of human remains from the church's cemetery).

In another modification to the 1876 event, the mayor and city hall reviewed the procession, a formal expression of the growing power of the office. While today this seems perfunctory, this was the first time such a thing was done in New Haven, reflecting the status of mayors who no longer came from the ranks of Yale-educated scholars but rather were men whose professions, most often as successful business leaders, were themselves formalized over the course of the nineteenth century. It would be hard to imagine New Haven's first mayor, the plainspoken and plainly dressed "Puritan politician" Roger Sherman, situating himself as the formal viewer of a parade, which might account for the unusual arrangement of the ranks in the 1788 parade discussed in part II.

These changes aside, the most blatantly secular addition to the procession was the presence of "several companies of antique and horrible fantastics," which were expected to "add much to the festivities of the occasion." The antiques and horribles were a rowdy bunch and illustrate, more than anything else, the change in tone in this celebration from earlier events. New Haveners wearing "grotesque" costumes, acting out ludicrous burlesques and displaying curious inscriptions and banners, were accompanied by the sounds of horns, kettledrums, shouting and jokes. This part of the procession, which incredibly started at the early hour of 6:30 a.m., was headed by a "pioneer in a fancy hairy suit, carrying an immense axe eight feet long." There followed one bawdy burlesque group after another, including a performance in parody of the New Haven police force, where "patrolmen carried champagne bottles instead of billy clubs" and "General Beeswax" on horseback led twenty "Broadway ghosts," also on horseback. These characters, including "Fitzhugh Wiggins" and his seventy-five men, were "carried in antiquated vehicles and ancient chaises." One "Columbian" (Native American?), supposedly captured at Fort Ticonderoga, was seen, as were the Terribles of Sandy Hollow (from Wards 1 and 10 in the city) and, finally, the Whangdoodles, who were clowns in old Continental uniforms. Pulling up the rear was the Wreck of the *Mayflower* group, with "relics" of the vessel being sold along the parade route at "fifty cents a hunk." With a tinge of irony, the *Register* reported that the "Mayflower was followed by a yellow chaise one hundred and twenty years of age, and the worst ever seen in this city." New Haveners, knowing their city to be a center for carriage making in New England, would have understood the allusion.

As though these sights were not enough, more horribles came out later, this time in three groups from different parts of the city: the Dragons of Fair Haven (who carried a banner with a picture of a "hideous" dragon), the Grand Centrals and the Hotchkisstown Invincibles of Westville. Then "Horrible Bill from Clam Town" appeared, as well as another banner with a picture of a giant clam and the words "The pride of the Town." When Americans think of grotesques, horrible and fantastics from the nineteenth century, Bridgeport resident P.T. Barnum is likely not far behind. Sure enough, Barnum made a donation to the celebration, which, according to the *Register*, was "an old wagon on the roof of which were a caged rooster and cat and in which several human representatives and monkeys and 'what is its' was greeted with great laughter along the line." An older couple called the Elm City Twins were seen in the procession, possessed "of terrible demeanor," and finally, "a pair of oxen pulled up the rear drawing one of the revolutionary carriages and containing worthy patriarchs." The banners carried in this part of the parade were similarly teasing. The *Register* described one "old lady in fantastic bloomer costume of many colors" carrying a sign reading, "May I vote?" while other banners were inscribed with the visages of two older people under the slogan, "Centennial Kisses." Unfortunately, their straining lips couldn't touch because their noses were far too long. One can only wonder what Reverend Bacon would have said if he had seen this display. As it was, he was there in 1876, just has he had been in 1838, but he was safely inside Center Church, preparing for his "historical oration."

At the services at Center Church at 2:00 p.m., Mayor Henry G. Lewis read President Ulysses S. Grant's Fourth of July proclamation, a scene that would be repeated one hundred years later when Mayor Frank Logue read President Gerald Ford's Fourth of July address. Another first for the American centennial celebration in New Haven was the focus on women in the orations. The Honorable E.K. Foster spoke "glowingly and earnestly of the great influence exerted by the women of America upon our social and political institutions. Whether those institutions were to endure another century depended largely…upon the wives and mothers of the republic." Finally, Reverend Bacon took his turn at the pulpit and provided the longest oration of the day, an overview of why Americans split from the British empire and what New Haven was like in 1776, ending his discourse with the Connecticut state motto, which is inscribed on the state flag: *Qui Transtulit Sustinet* ("He who transplanted still sustains").

In a strange confluence of programming, while Reverend Bacon was orating inside Center Church, a hot air balloon called the Eagle was

Opposite: Program, Centennial Celebration, 1776–1876. Published by C.M. Loomis, 1876. *Courtesy of Joseph Taylor. Photograph by Jessica Zielonka.*

going up, with throngs of "struggling, perspiring humanity" on Church and Chapel Streets trying to get a look. Apparently, people were making so much noise outside that many people got up and left the oration to see what was going on. Upon walking out of the doors of Center Church, they would have seen Professor Fisher's "rise in the world," which was scheduled for 3:00 p.m. (though it didn't ascend until about thirty minutes later). The *Register* reported that the balloon "went up with a bound, with the aeronaut clinging to the frail basket with one hand and waving his hat with the other." Missing all the trees, the balloon and the aeronaut rose very high and were taken by the wind in a northeasterly direction, finally landing in Higganum, Connecticut, though Professor Fisher returned to New Haven to receive his accolades. And this was only the first balloon of the day. In the evening, a "fire balloon" was sent up, though with much less success.

As at the 1838 event, New Haven schoolchildren were again a major part of the festivities. Under the direction of Professor Benjamin Jepson, regarded as one of the first music teachers in the United States, "2,800 children of the public schools…were to give a great concert on the public square." While students had paraded and cheered in the earlier New Haven celebrations, this time students from the city's eight public schools were "dressed and arranged as to represent the American flag," singing "Yankee Doodle," "My Country, 'Tis of Thee," "Rally Round the Flag," "Glory Hallelujah" and "The Star-Spangled Banner." The number of so many "standard" American songs was reflective of the continuing development of American nationalism, which also appeared in the roleplaying undertaken by students. Female high school students dressed as the "Goddess of Liberty" (there was no Statue of Liberty in New York Harbor until 1886), while the boys dressed as colonials and colonials playing "Indians" in a re-creation of the Boston Tea Party. There were processions, orations, a balloon, singing, antiques, horribles and, finally, something a little more permanent: the laying of cornerstone for an addition to Germania Hall on Wooster Street, which held the German English School and its society, the Teutonic Menner Chor. In the cavity of the cornerstone was placed a tin box with copies of the newspapers of the day, the *Evening Register*, a list of members of both societies and a list of the building committee members, scholars from the school and the board of education members.

This day in New Haven, like many summer days in New England, was scorching. The *Register* noted that "the Green was covered with people, and the proprietors of booths and ice cream saloons were reaping an immense harvest." The night hours brought little relief, but likely everyone's attention was captured by the illuminations. Well in advance of electricity, the emphasis on illumination at the centennial was made by coordinating bonfires (called "beacon fires"), gaslights and different types of fireworks, including the much anticipated "fire balloon," which rose from the Green. Fireworks were supposed to explode from the fire balloon, but it ended in "one grand disappointing fizzle." Apparently, the fireworks actually became dislodged from the balloon and "burst right and left into the multitudes." No one was fatally injured, but one boy was struck in the stomach and taken to a doctor's office. Another source of centennial illuminations were the beacon fires set on the surrounding hills, including Bethany Hills and West Rock. The *Register* described the New Haven nighttime scene from the top of a downtown building:

> *The shimmering of the waters of the harbor, under the mellow light of a full moon, the Chinese lanterns glowing through the open spaces and glimmering through the leaves, the illuminated buildings, the beacon fires, numerous rockets and roman candles, and the thousands of gay people moving hither and thither made a sight that will not be witnessed here again for some time to come, if at all.*

The program of fireworks was the finale to the American centennial celebration in New Haven, which, it was reported, "looked better on paper than it appeared to the actual eyewitnesses." Apparently, what was promised was extensive, "but in quality there was a said deficiency."

There were troubles at this huge event: the searing temperatures, the daylight that would not cooperate with the illuminations, the injured boy, the disappointing fireworks and the arguments (the Governor's Foot Guard, whose members were asked to participate but wouldn't, sat inside Grand Army Hall while the activities proceeded). If anything, the *Register*'s account of the Centennial Celebration is a reminder that people in 1876 toiled with many of the same exertions and challenges that we do. The *Register* ended its coverage of the event with the sentiment of "the almost universal exclamation of the wearied sight-seers: well, I'm glad the Fourth is over with." Tired is the writer who ends with the assessment that, at least, the day was "free from deplorable events."

CENTENNIAL OF THE EVACUATION/INVASION OF NEW HAVEN, JULY 1879

We do not celebrate or glorify the invasion of New Haven by the British.
We do rejoice over the fact that the yeomancy of New Haven summarily
expelled an overwhelming force of British invaders.
        –New Haven Evening Register, *July 5, 1879*

New Haveners must have had powerful memories of the day forty-eight British vessels and three thousand soldiers anchored off West Haven's shore, intending a full-scale invasion on July 5, 1779. According to historian Michael Sletcher, the event, in which Britain launched a two-pronged invasion from East Haven and West Haven into downtown, was aided by New Haven Loyalists (those enemies so often mentioned in newspapers of the time). Many people fled to the countryside, but many others stayed. Some twenty-seven residents died (interesting to note that no monument or memorial exists to these people, some of whom were bayoneted, and one epileptic man, Elisha Tuttle, had his tongue cut out and later died from the wound). The invasion resulted in the net loss of little material wealth as compared to other towns that were burned such as Norwalk and Fairfield, and the British returned to New York City the next day, perhaps satisfied with the burning of the town's ordnance (gunpowder) and general marauding. While many New Haveners fled, many others stayed to fight the British (including a visiting Aaron Burr), and thus this brief episode presented to New Haven another opportunity to celebrate its role in the Revolutionary War. The 1879 Centennial Celebration is a good example of how history is rewritten as needed, when needed, as generations well past that July 5 in 1779 were able to recast the event to fit the desire of their time. New Haven would not be cast as victim of the invaders but as a force that turned the British out.

The *New Haven Evening Register* on July 3, 1879, stated as much: "We do not celebrate or glorify the invasion of New Haven by the British. We do rejoice over the fact that the yeomancy of New Haven summarily expelled an overwhelming force of British invaders." Thus, for nineteenth-century New Haveners (and the reverberations lasting into the twentieth century, with the 1979 reenactment), it was the *evacuation* of New Haven, not the *invasion* of New Haven. The engraving done for the cover of the accompanying memorial booklet reinforces the reworked history: a line of ships sails away from land (New Haven), on which a female figure (Lady Liberty or

Two objects, both associated with Ezra Stiles, exist from the day New Haven was invaded by the British (July 5, 1779). Most well known is the map of the invasion that Stiles drew in his diary (which has been reproduced countless times), but there is also this telescope. Ezra Stiles, the president of Yale College, took his spyglass to the Yale College Athenaeum tower and viewed small "boats pulling off from the ships and landing a little after sunrise." Made by Banks of London, circa 1780, the authenticity of this "looking glass" as the one used by Stiles is not beyond reproach, but it is an attractive example of telescopes of the period. Called an "improved 30 inch telescope," the dimensions when set up for use are length 72.5 cm, width 33.0 cm, height 42.5 cm. *Courtesy of the Yale Peabody Museum of Natural History, YPM HSI 010403.*

perhaps the personification of New Haven) holds a book in her right hand titled *History*, and with the pointing finger on her left hand, she directs our attention to the word "Evacuation." A classical column, on which sits a stoic bald eagle, divides the fleeing British ships from Liberty. The *Evening Register* helped in this endeavor, stating that "she rained bullets upon the British in such copious showers, that they quailed before the storms and fled their boats for safety." In his 2004 book *New Haven: From Puritanism to the Age of Terror*, Michael Sletcher wrote that the British did no such thing. "[B]y

Memorial of the Centennial Celebration of the Evacuation of New Haven, 1879, program book published by Punderson & Crisand, Lithographers and Printers, 12 Center Street, New Haven. *Courtesy of the Whitney Library, New Haven Museum. Photograph by Jessica Zielonka.*

noon the British were in complete control of the town and many soldiers proceeded to get drunk, pillaging and terrorizing the inhabitants of New Haven." As the saying goes, history is written by the victor—although in this case, history can be rewritten if the victor is far enough away and enough time has passed.

The centennial of the evacuation of New Haven was put together by a special committee of the city council, historical society and private citizens. The daylong program had the usual celebratory parts: the ringing of bells, the firing of the national salute at sunrise, a reception held by the Second Regiment Governor's Foot Guard, a grand military and civic parade at 11:00 a.m., military parades on the Green in the early afternoon and, at 4:00 p.m., another one of Reverend Bacon's historical orations at Center Church (he had been doing this regularly since the second centennial in 1838). Finally, there was a thirty-eight-gun salute at sunset for the thirty-eight states, a band concert on the Green and also another at Wooster Square by the American Band.

The 1879 memorial booklet captures the size of the parade by listing all of the marching divisions, a reminder of how important collective participation was for Americans and that New Haven was a draw in the region. The first division of the parade, the military, had regimental marchers from Waterbury, Meriden, Middletown, Norwalk, Bridgeport, Guilford and Hartford, with more men from Boston, Cambridge, Newton and Medford. The second division, the fire departments, was equally large and had participants from Ansonia, South Norwalk, Middletown, Stratford and Waterbury. Much of this division was devoted to the display of "Old Hand Engines," with the earliest engine going back to 1819, and "antique firemen, representing the old styles of uniforms." At the end, there was even a twenty-nine-year-old horse named "Old Major" that had been in service for twenty years. The July 5, 1879 edition of the *Register* reported, "The Old Fashioned Bucket Company of thirty men was something quite novel, and appeared to deeply interest the spectators. The uniform was cocked hat, turkey-red coat, black trousers and white belts. The buckets were carried on suspended poles…it was this section that represented the red shirts and black trousers that used to be so conspicuous at fire parades."

In the eighth division of the procession marched the trades, which included nine New Haven companies: two carriage makers, a paperhanger, a grocery, a printing press and a piano maker. Also in this was the *Col. J.H. Starin*, a "handsome model of a Steamboat on wheels." The inclusion of local businesses in celebrations such as this is a sign of the times, with the Phillips Steam Marble and Granite Works in the lead. Businesses made their appearance, but there was less emphasis on New Haven's civic societies, although the Germans themselves formed the whole fourth division. The *Register* reported, "[T]he German societies presented an exhibition such as every German heart loves…embowered in evergreens…one wagon bore a representation of a boar hunt…the German division was well sprinkled with the flag of Germany." New Haven's massive nineteenth-century German population has left little mark on the landscape of the city today. Unlike the Irish and Italian communities, which still retain cultural toeholds through bakeries, restaurants, historical societies, monuments, churches and festivals, German American culture in New Haven exists only in the archives.

For the first time in any publication created for a New Haven celebration, "points of historical interest" were included. Historic homes in New Haven were the focus, including the location of Benedict Arnold and Roger Sherman's homes; the demolished homes of Davenport, Eaton and Nathan Beers ("brutally murdered by the British"); and General Wooster's home on Wooster Street. One wonders if the emphasis on historic houses trickled into New Haven consciousness due to the work of the Mount Vernon Ladies Association—the first historic preservation group, which was already hard at work saving George Washington's home in Virginia.

The late nineteenth-century practice of intertwining business, marketing and culture is exposed in an advertisement (from Norton & Company, Clothiers, 375 Chapel Street) that appeared in the *New Haven Evening Register* on July 5, 1879:

> *Everybody is preparing for the great Day of Jubilee and Jolification, when our handsome city (the Paradise of New England), will wear an apparel of beauty. One hundred thousand people from far and near will enjoy the festivities of the most auspicious event chronicled in the history of the City of Four Thousand Elms. With Progress written on our Banner, and with Sentiments of Patriotism THE GREAT CLOTHIERS extend a hearty welcome to Strangers who are to join our townspeople in the glorious celebration…*
>
> *In addition to the regular programme for Independence Week, the ENTHUSIASTIC CLOTHIERS will entertain thousands of citizens who will invade Oak Hall, THE GREAT CLOTHING RENDEVOUS of New Haven, and compel our little army of Salesmen to surrender fifty thousand dollars' worth of men's and boy's clothing!*

In the twentieth century, the evacuation of New Haven was renamed the invasion of New Haven, but the reenactments often took the shape of the 1879 narrative. This happened at the Yale Pageant in 1916, in the Connecticut state tercentenary in 1935 and in the New Haven tercentenary's historical pageant (the first scene was called "The Advance of the British," with the second scene called "The Retreat of the British"). Finally, in 1979, there was a large-scale reenactment at Lighthouse Point and Black Rock Fort, although here, according to the *New Haven Register*, the "British Army [Reigns] Supreme Once Again in Battle."

CENTENNIAL OF THE INCORPORATION OF THE CITY, FOURTH OF JULY 1884

The pearly drops came in showers and they washed and rinsed the smoked and powder-filled air.
–New Haven Evening Register, *July 5, 1884*

It rained the evening of the Fourth of July 1884, which marked another Centennial Celebration in New Haven: the 100th anniversary of the year in which New Haven became incorporated as a city and Roger Sherman was installed as the city's first mayor. It was reported in the *New Haven Evening Register* on July 1 that money had run out for the celebration, and therefore plans had to be altered. Original plans for beacon fires were nixed, with fireworks substituted, and the national salute was done from the top of East Rock Park instead of the "old green," to which the *Register* commented that "it is doubtful if anyone knew the inspiring salvos of freedom were being fired." Other cities, such as New York, had been incorporated under the British empire, but according to the *Register*, this was "the first instance in which one of the United States acting in its own independent and sovereign capacity granted a city charter." The day after the event, the newspaper helped its readers understand the significance of the centennial of incorporation:

This event has real connections with the Declaration of Independence, for the growth of cities has been one of the most remarkable and important features of the extraordinary development of the nation which came into being July 4, 1776 for upon the life of its cities depends in large measure the life of the nation…the cities therefore, hold the future of the nation in their control: with them is the weal or woe of this majestic republic. Not, then, as a light or trifling thing do we remember the first incorporation of a city in the United States.

Except for a few small changes, the celebration followed the usual form. The *Constitution* was put at the head of the four-mile-long parade, which was reported to be as large as 125,000 people, thus earning the title "largest celebration ever" in New Haven (Monument Day eclipsed this event three years later). Brought out for another appearance was the procession of antiques and horribles, this time led by Jewell's Two Paw Circus (a "great Yankee, English, German, Irish and American museum and menagerie"), consisting of five cages "filled with animals and other living curiosities." The *Register* reported on July 1 that 400 people planned to march with the antiques and horribles, whose carriages were described as "the wheels of the vehicles are decorated with ribbons and strings of all colors and degrees of cleanliness…the sides of the cages are trimmed with small flags." Because New Haveners joined in Jewell's Two Paw Circus, many of the curiosities came from New Haven itself, including a "sacred elephant" that was "imported from a Chapel Street dry goods store for 85 cents" and the "excelsior circus from Oak Street." Pulled by oxen, the elephant was put together with muslin over a four-foot-long wooden frame and was "laughable to the extreme." Also appearing in this celebration was the new municipal flag for New Haven, described as "blue with white field containing city shield and Connecticut grapevines."

One serious note crept into the *Register*'s reporting, demonstrating the importance that the idea of the "city" as a formal structure had become to New Haven:

> *The right government of cities in a republic is the greatest problem which now faces us. We are not yet a large enough city to feel greatly the pressure of this problem upon ourselves, but its shadow is already over us, and if our growth and prosperity continue we shall soon have to face it in all the magnitude. And it can only be met successfully by all good citizens giving their first interest to municipal affairs.*

In addition, another challenge arising out of the second half of the nineteenth century was the ever-increasing diversification of New Haven's population, about which the *Register* commented:

> *The most marked difference between the New Haven of 1784 and the same city in 1884 is the increase of population. But hardly less marked than this is the change in the character of the population…today almost half our population is foreign born or the children of foreign parents. And here we touch upon the cause of the marvelous development of the city and*

of the nation…we have been made strong and great by the vast flood of immigration…and we have welcomed them and made them our brethren and fellow citizens and they are no more aliens among us.

The issues that came to the fore around the city's "semi-centennial" in 1888 (250th anniversary) were reported heavily by the *Register* only four years later, suggesting that tension between groups of people in the Elm City was no longer something that could be ignored or placated with such soothing sentiments.

FOUNDERS' DAY: 250TH ANNIVERSARY OF NEW HAVEN, APRIL 1888

We are all the better to-day for having blown our little horn yesterday, albeit we blew it modestly and within the limits of the town.
—*"Yesterday's Celebration,"* New Haven Evening Register,
April 26, 1888

New Haven's 250th anniversary came quickly on the heels of two other large events in the Elm City in the 1880s: the centennial of incorporation in 1884 and the tremendous dedication celebration for the Soldiers and Sailors Monument at the top of East Rock Park in 1887. New Haven chose a much different tone for the 250th anniversary, calling the event "Founders' Day" and purportedly laying the emphasis on Reverend John Davenport. The *New Haven Evening Register* wrote of the event, "We do not remember an occasion which was prepared with less bluster and noisy advertising… everything was undertaken modestly but thoroughly." There were to be no antiques and horribles in this parade. The first planning meeting for the 250th anniversary was December 22, 1887, at Loomis' Temple of Music. On the outsized committee composed of 105 men were 4 members of the New Haven Colony Historical Society, itself only a twenty-six-year-old organization. From here, the committee determined that it needed more funds for the event, and a special town meeting was called on March 15, 1888, when the anniversary was formally titled Founders' Day and $2,000 was appropriated from city funds.

Though the Founders' Day event "passed off today in an orderly, dignified manner, in keeping with the character of the event it commemorated," according to the *New Haven Evening Register* on April 25, 1888, there were changes to this celebration from earlier ones, reflecting the huge shift in the structure of New Haven's commercial and civic life in the fifty years between 1838 and 1888. For the general public, the event seemed to hold little real interest or attraction; the *Register* reported, "Probably the number of people who manifested a deep interest in the day was somewhat limited, and was confined to those who took part in a similar occasion fifty years ago. But it was a holiday and it gave everybody a chance to be seen." Why such little enthusiasm for the celebration? Were New Haveners just plain exhausted from the previous celebrations in 1884 and 1887, or was there something else going on in the life of the Elm City that offers an explanation? Certainly, a lack of funds and volunteers was not the issue, nor, probably, the city's organizing of yet another celebration; there is no mention in the extensive coverage of the event provided by the *New Haven Evening Register* that people were tired of the act of celebrating. In other words, the planning committee went through its paces mechanically, as if the members knew that they *should* do it, and therefore did it, but without much enthusiasm, or style.

So, while the second centennial in 1838 created the archetype for anniversary celebrations in New Haven, and the American centennial in 1876 went for spectacle, Founders' Day in 1888 was more important for the issues raised around different parts of the celebration and not necessarily for the form of the event itself. Uncertainty and tension in New Haven may provide some explanation—the mixing of beliefs about the past and ideas for the present/future, for example. The continuing enlargement of ethnic groups and the heightened prominence of commercial interests via the city's burgeoning manufacturing businesses were also factors. In many ways, Founders' Day is familiar to us. It looks and sounds like an event from the twenty-first century. Lip service is paid to societal problems, but real emotion or sentiment is missing.

For example, the organizers seemed torn between a reverence for the past (with the focus on John Davenport; the opening hymn, music and printed program were all purposefully "ancient," done in the style of 250 years earlier) and a belief in progress, which, though usually tied together in American culture as two sides of the same coin, was a source of tension. This was not the case during New Haven's 1938 tercentenary, when the "past" was packaged effectively into the face of a jolly Puritan and marketed through an explosion of visual materials, impressed onto every segment of life in the Elm City. That kind of wholehearted belief in progress was plainly suggested in 1838, as we saw in Hezakiah Auger's medal, which prominently displayed the insertion of modern technology into the Elm City. But it was not progress in the form of powerful new technologies that was notable in 1888; rather, the addition of commercial practices that accompanied the escalation of manufacturing was a new part of the anniversary celebrations.

One stanza from a poem titled "Quin-nippe-ohke," published on Founders' Day in the *New Haven Evening Register*, gives a sense of the cultural change:

> *For we have reached a higher plane*
> *Of dealing and of way.*
> *And he who gets the most for naught*
> *Receives the loudest praise.*
> *The golden rule is absolute*
> *In business now, you know*
> *But 'twas not two hundred*
> *And fifty years ago.*

Tellingly, the New Haven Chamber of Commerce makes its first appearance in anniversary celebrations during Founders' Day. About 150 members marched in the procession, and that evening, a dinner was held at Loomis' Temple of Music, which received coverage in the *Register*. The chamber was described in the April 26, 1888 edition as "the practical business men of this city, regardless of religion or politics, are banded together in one organization for the patriotic purpose of making the most of the opportunities given them to carry on the work of progress and civilization which their forefathers and fathers did so well in their time and generation." Founded in 1794, the New Haven Chamber of Commerce had started small, but its growing status in the Elm City was apparent: "It was no longer pertinent or humorous to ask what the chamber did between meals. The question was now, when does the chamber find time to eat?" At this dinner, the *Register* reported that Timothy Dwight, the president of Yale University, was the center of attention, with many men joking that if Dwight could run for the presidency of the United States, "he may not be a politician but he would be acceptable to New Haven."

As in anniversary celebrations past, local businesses were asked to close during the program hours, but for the first time, notice was given in the newspaper that "there is a movement on foot to have the banks close on Founders' Day and many manufacturers will close their shops to give their employees a chance to celebrate." It was also reported that Meyer Zunder (after whom a school would be named) appointed a committee to confer with the wholesale houses on State Street, and they agreed to close at 11:00 a.m. The closing of the post office is also mentioned.

One of the conversations at this dinner highlights the tension between past and present/future in New Haven, via the fate of the statehouse (also called "the noble pile") on the Green. One chamber member got up to say:

> *She* [New Haven] *owns the only state house in the possession of any city in the United States.* [Laughter] *There is the impression that I do not love the state house. I do love the old relic…newspaper articles have convinced me that the old state house cannot be repaired for town, city or private purposes. The people of New Haven have decided that the state house cannot be demolished. Therefore we enjoy the singular distinction of having a state house that cannot be repaired or demolished.*

Though the comment was made in jest, the dichotomy between reverence for the past and belief in progress is put into further relief when the Founders' Day medal is considered. The statehouse appears on the medal on the reverse, nestled among the elms trees with its pediment showing, but it survived only one more year and was torn down in 1889. New Haven is familiar with the vexing twentieth-century issues raised from the tearing down of whole neighborhoods during heightened moments of "progress," such as the years of redevelopment in the 1950s and 1960s, but the tearing down of a landmark such as the statehouse is a reflection of its moment too. The *Boston Advertiser* editorialized in 1889 that the New Haven Statehouse was a "priceless momento of the glorious past"—not exactly what some in New Haven wanted to hear. The *Register* shot back:

> *It will be news to most New Haveners to be told that the House is a "priceless momento of the glorious past." It is not and has never been priceless. It is a momento of New Haven's folly in allowing Hartford to gobble up the capital. It is a perfect reminder that New Haven in the past has shown a deplorable lack of public spirit in important crises. It is not a "chief milestone on the path of time." Rather is it an encumbrance, a public nuisance, a bone of contention, an eyesore, a laughing stock, a hideous pile of brick and mortar, a blot on the fair surface of the Green. The Boston paper doesn't know what it is talking about.*

The tension between reverence and progress are again illuminated when both sides of the medal are viewed in the context of New Haven's interests in the 1880s. As we have seen, the growth of commercial and manufacturing enterprises has become a central tenet to the core of New Haven identity, but how did the city bring this into line with its Puritan heritage, specifically during the city's 250th anniversary, which was purported to be focused on the founders? In fact, there was little focus on the founders during the event itself, and while the *Register* wrote that "we should not be afraid to take them out of the gilded frames history has placed them in and lay them on the dissecting table," next to nothing of this was done. Instead, summations of New Haven past and present were spoken, and poems extolling the virtues of Davenport and Eaton were published ("Led on by Davenport the wise, and Eaton strong and true").

The engraver of the Founders' Day medal was C. Theiler, who was based in Cleveland, Ohio, though the medal was probably produced in Meriden, Connecticut. It is not known if Theiler was also the designer or if he only did the engraving. Either way, it is clear that the artist was not as accomplished as Hezekiah Auger, either in creating the design or in the technical work. Like Auger, Theiler divided the surface into two registers with a horizontal band, with a larger upper half showing, uniquely, a bird's-eye view of the Green (the artist's application of perspective is intuitive, not scientific). Once again, the tree cover is emphasized, as are the churches, Yale buildings, the tower of Henry Austin's city hall (built in 1861) and, as discussed earlier, the statehouse. A feature in the center of the Green is the massive liberty pole from which different flags were hung, as it was the central spot for celebrations. An oval- or lozenge-shaped insert in the bottom register is further divided into two registers featuring the symbols of the arts and humanities, together with the iron forge that, like the similar iron forge used in the Institute Library's bookplate, is a sign of self-improvement (the city

Founders' Day medal, C. Theiler, engraver, bronze, 1888, 2001.87.27963. *Courtesy of the Yale University Art Gallery, transfer from the Sterling Memorial Library, Yale University.*

is always striving to improve, the one concession to the idea of progress depicted on the medal) and the mechanical arts that flourished from the beginnings laid by Eli Whitney at the turn of the century.

On the reverse of the medal is a repeat of Auger's 1838 medal, with Reverend John Davenport preaching under the oak. The figures, carved with much less detail, appear in a horizontal line, with one figure kneeling in prayer next to a bush. The Quinnipiac Indians are now banished from the scene, and the view of East Rock appears as part of the trap rock ridge. Though encouraged otherwise by the *Register*, coincidentally the scene is placed in a rectangular frame, lending a historical flavor. Above and attached to the picture frame is a bust of Reverend John Davenport, the head copied from the well-known circa 1670 painting of Davenport owned by the Yale University Art Gallery (seen on page 24). Overall, this visual representation of what was important to New Haven in 1888 is a retread of an earlier idea and fails to capture any real feeling for the moment. To add insult to injury, the planning committee decided that a medal would not be part of its work, and thus "no medal was struck by the general committee to commemorate the celebration, but Mr. Theiler of Meriden was authorized to make one as a matter of private enterprise." Thus, the medal that was produced was not commissioned nor sanctioned by the planning committee, which may have contributed to its lackluster sales as the *Register* also tells us that "the manufacturer of the Founders' Day medals had appointed Henry Peck sole agent for their sale" and that "medal vendors were everywhere, but apparently their trade was not brisk." A Founders' Day badge was also produced, as were silk ribbons, most likely worn by different groups processing.

These problems were joined by the addition of veiled hostility between ethnic groups—the first time such issues are mentioned in the context of anniversary celebrations in New Haven. According to the April 12, 1888 issue of the *New Haven Evening Register*, "as usual, when any public event or celebration is prepared for in New Haven race prejudice has stepped in and interfered with the universality of the Founders' Day exercises." The rapid growth in New Haven immigrant populations during the second half of the nineteenth century meant that new relationships between different groups of people had sparked argument over public space. The headline from that issue tells us something about the different ethnic groups vying for space in the Elm City at the end of the nineteenth century: "Not Specifically Invited: Englishmen Will Not Parade."

According to the article, the "English societies" (which included the Sons of St. George, the Naturalization Society and the Crocker Club) and the "Scotch Societies" (the Caledonian Club and Clara MacLeod) refused to participate in the march because in a letter directed to one New Haven civic leader, the

Founders' Day badge, 1888, 2001.87.27071. *Courtesy of the Yale University Art Gallery, transfer from the Sterling Memorial Library, Yale University.*

chief marshal of the parade, General S.R. Smith, asked him specifically to encourage "every large local society of the city, and principle among the largest civic societies are the A.O.H, temperance and others of the Irish people." That is, Smith's focus on the Irish in New Haven put the noses of the Anglo-Scotch out of joint, and they voted to not participate. When called on to explain their position, the *Evening Register* reported the weak answers given by a member of the British American club: "[N]early every man in the club voted against parading simple because he hadn't any anxiety to tramp through the street…we voted not to parade because we [do] not believe in parades." However, a Scotch club member gave an equally lame response, saying that they would not parade because they had no regalia or uniforms. General Smith, the chief marshal of the parade, resigned the next day.

Five days later, the *Evening Register* reported that the British American club had held a meeting at which the parade was discussed, and according to a club member who spoke to the *Evening Register* reporter, "not a word was said against the Irish—not one word." The protest sounds hollow, especially when the *Evening Register* further reported on a resolution that supported the mayor when he removed an Irish flag on display at city hall. According to the same club member as reported in the paper, "it should not be inferred from our resolution that we singled out the Irish flag for such a resolution." Such actions, read together, indicate that there were, in fact, real problems.

Another view of Founders' Day involves the presence of two Native Americans, neither of whom were Quinnipiacs. Two "Indians" named Dr. John

Jomah and Lilia Jomah contacted the planning committee with a proposal: "It would add greatly to the interest of the parade if real live Indians were in the procession." The committee agreed and appropriated five dollars of its funds to the Jomahs, who would either ride horses or ride in carriages. The *Evening Register* reported that they "are said to have come to this city to sell medicine." That part of the story could have easily been true, although the "Indian" part was sometimes a fabrication of place and culture.

The next day, the *Evening Register* reported on "Mrs. Jomah's Hard Story," which combined elements from western Native American culture mixed with a heavy dose of storytelling drawn from the stereotypes already codified in the Euro-American imagination about Native Americans. (In the *Evening Register* issue on Founders' Day, an advertisement for "Kirk's White Cloud Floating Soap," with an image of a Native American man labeled "The Chief" appeared; these kinds of images were ubiquitous in American marketing.) The Jomahs, claiming that they were from a Six Nations tribe (Iroqouis/Haudenosaunee) of central/upstate New York, told the *Evening Register* that a buffalo hide was used by the "bad white man [in New Haven] to swindle poor Lo out of his land by means of sharp tricks" and that "he got the Indians to ratify the contract by giving them bad whiskey." The long tales told by the Jomahs became longer when they claimed that an earlier tribe existed in New Haven called the Shawebas. Clearly eager to please, the Jomahs also offered to tell the "story of Minnehaha" at the Founders' Day event while "attired in Indian costumes."

This mixing of cultural traditions—there is no historic figure named Minnehaha, only the female character from the fabulously popular Romantic poem "Song of Hiawatha" penned by Henry Wadsworth Longfellow in 1855—gives us some insight into New Haven's disconnect with its own Native American heritage. One wonders if the committee members regretted their decision to pay the Jomahs five dollars and invite them to participate in the event or if they and their stories were viewed as quaint or appealing, much like the "antiques and horribles" on display in earlier celebrations. This is the first New Haven event in which Native Americans participated, yet Quinnipiac Indians, who were thought by the white population to be extinct, were there, living on the margins of society "as they did in other locales in New England," according to John Menta. "[T]he indigenous survivors kept such a low profile that they lived virtually unnoticed by their white neighbors." In other words, it did not even cross the minds of the planning committee that the "founders" of Founders' Day in New Haven might include Quinnipiacs or other local Native Americans. Whether or not

Quinnipiac descendants were around didn't matter; they were, in the words of historian Jean O'Brien, written out of Elm City history.

It turns out that there were more "Indians" marching in the parade, under the second division (civic societies), but these were seventy-five "braves" from the Improved Order of Red Men. The *Evening Register* wrote of these white men dressed as Native Americans, "the real Indians [the Lomahs], who were a leading feature, it must be said, could not hold a candle to the painted, feathered and much-bedecked specimens of the improved order." Even the "real" Native Americans could not live up to the stereotype of the "brave"; whites preferred them "savage looking in their Indian garments and with dangerous appearing weapons…some were on horseback, some on foot and all noisy with the boisterous Indian Whoop, which to the great amusement of the small boy, could be heard blocks away." The Knights of Columbus followed the Improved Order of Red Men, with their historical tableaux car of the "Landing of Christopher Columbus." In 1888, there was no irony to be seen in the Red Men/Columbus combination.

The position in New Haven toward Native Americans in 1888 was sentimentalized in a long poem titled "Quin-nippe-ohke," published in the *Evening Register* on Founders' Day by William Pinney. The stanzas concerned with the Native Americans in Greater New Haven read:

And then and there Quinnipeeohks,
"Long water place" was bought,
We know not what the white man paid,
Or what the red man sought,
But white men in those days were true,
And honest, this we know,
Remember 'twas two hundred
And fifty years ago.

'Tis well those brave old chiefs of old
Met not upon the way
A delegation of such men
As we shall know today;
For if they had I sadly fear
Fair treatment would lack,
And luck had they been to save
The blankets on their backs.

Also not a part of the 1888 celebration was Reverend Leonard Bacon, who had died in 1881. His spirit was invoked though during the anniversary services in Center Church: "[W]ith many of you his name will be oftenest on your lips to-day, and his spirit seems to belong to the whole history of this people." There was also a reading of "Dr. Bacon's Hymn." The president of Yale College, Timothy Dwight, took the lead during the 1888 celebrations, and his involvement on the Founders' Day planning committee meant that Yale played a larger role in the event than previously seen. Yale opened its Alumni Hall to the public for the day, and the portrait of John Davenport, the sword of General Wooster and "other interesting relics" were put on exhibition. The historical oration (traditionally given by Bacon) was provided by Reverend Dr. Newman Smyth, while Reverend Dr. Reed would do the same at Trinity—the first time another church on the Green is mentioned as part of celebrations. Other churches in New Haven also offered special sermons, including Reverend E.S. Lewis of St. Paul's, Dr. Twitchell at Dwight Place and Reverend Dr. Chapman at First Methodist.

The Founders' Day celebration in 1888 was snow-covered, with the *Evening Register* writing, "It is doubtful if John Davenport ever saw so much snow on any April 25th he ever spent here." The banks of snow provided impromptu viewing platforms for the 10:30 a.m. procession (which was a far cry from the 6:30 a.m. start time for the 1876 event). New to this event was the participation of the New Haven Bicycle Club at sixty-five members strong. The *Evening Register* does not say if they were on bicycles or not, though one suspects not due to the snow.

Photograph, blizzard of 1888, New Haven. Note the red and white painted liberty pole in the center of the Green. *Courtesy of Joseph Taylor.*

As befits a business-driven planning committee, the Founders' Day celebration committee had success with its budget, and in another break with the past, Eli Whitney Jr. published the final income and expense numbers in the newspaper, coming out ahead with $787.13 in unused funds (not having fireworks saved money). With an eye toward longevity, the committee also published a booklet about the event on May 14, 1888, and even began plans for a new monument to be installed in the to-be-renamed Monument Square, a sliver of land at the juncture of Congress, Church, Meadow and George Streets. It is not surprising that the committee discussed erecting a bronze figure that "will represent a Puritan in correct garb," as Augustus St. Gaudens's *The Puritan* had been unveiled to great acclaim in Springfield, Massachusetts, in 1887. Again, though, the committee's dedicatory choice was odd; Theophilus Eaton—and not John Davenport—was named the subject of choice because "the memory of [him] is perhaps the most entitled to perpetuation and honor in this town, among whose founders he took so conspicuous a part. While Davenport and others deserted the town, Eaton

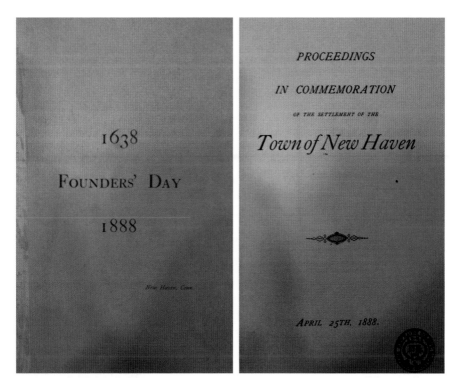

Proceedings in Commemoration of the Founding of the Settlement of New Haven, 1888. Courtesy of the Whitney Library, New Haven Museum. Photograph by Jessica Zielonka.

Columbus Day ribbon and badge, 1974.4.1. The 400th anniversary of Columbus Day was celebrated in New Haven on October 11, 1892. *Courtesy of the Knights of Columbus Museum. Photograph by the Knights of Columbus Museum and Jessica Zielonka.*

remained to witness the growth of the experiment of its founding." Though Reverend John Davenport was featured as the only founder on the Founders' Day medal, Eaton, always described as the New Haven Colony's government and business leader, was the figure who would get the monument.

The *Evening Register* reported that funds were to be raised by subscription, with "the plan…to execute the details while the history which Founders' Day commemorated is fresh in the people's minds." New Haven never did receive its Puritan monument, but a bronze tablet was installed in the "west wall of the brick store at the corner of College and George Street." That building was razed, and the last known location of the tablet came in 1977 from the New Haven Redevelopment Agency, which knew that the owner of the building had taken the tablet with him when he moved to Florida. His whereabouts at the time were unknown.

The final blowout celebration in New Haven at the end of the nineteenth century was the 400th anniversary of the landing of Columbus. Due to space limitations, this event and the previously mentioned Monument Day in 1887 (both of which were centered on monuments in New Haven) have been marginalized in this study, but they are very much part of the continuum of evolving celebrations in the Elm City. While Monument Day was probably the largest event the city has ever seen, this first Columbus Day event, sponsored by six Italian societies, drew forty thousand people to the New Haven Green to watch the six thousand Knights and thirty-six marching bands march. A monument to Columbus was installed in Wooster Square, and yearly celebrations are a New Haven tradition. Another major anniversary came around again in 1992, although this time it was called the Columbus 500 International. It purported to offer "an opportunity to come to terms with our past, shed old images and forge for ourselves a new national identity."

TREASURES FROM LATE NINETEENTH-CENTURY NEW HAVEN

New Haven's identity is tied to particular places, buildings, organizations and people, but everything is subject to change. People come and go, buildings are razed and new ones built, organizations fold and new ones take their place. In 2012, for example, the Hospital of St. Raphael merged with Yale–New

Haven Hospital; within a matter of days, all exterior signs were changed over to Yale blue, and a sense of place was altered. But St. Raph's story, like that of the Quinnipiac Indians or New Haven's German immigrants, doesn't end there. Reverberations are all around, if you develop your eyes to see them. The work that New Haven's museums, archives and libraries do to help us comprehend these reverberations is critical. There are stories behind stories behind stories for each one of these objects. New Haven's late nineteenth-century objects offer some of the richest material with which to work. Many scholars and theorists have questioned whether the study and presentation of objects in museums is desirable or even necessary in the twenty-first century. (Steven Conn explored these issues in his 2010 book *Do Museums Still Need Objects?*) After all, in our global, digitized, "open" societies, the emphasis is on the ability to share ideas across the clouds, to break free of any lingering hierarchical patrimony embedded in old institutions and old objects and to favor multitasking, independence and technology. But many museums have responded to these critiques, with some finding contemporary relevance and use in the power of objects.

Opposite, top: Shadowbox of Quinnipiac projectile points and other points. Quinnipiac Indians in New Haven were both written out of local history and, at the same time, romanticized through the marketing of images created from a blending of ideas. These kinds of displays are typical for late nineteenth-/early twentieth-century collections, in which "found" artifacts—the majority of which were not scientifically excavated but rather collected on the surface of the ground—are arranged to reinforce the symbols most closely associated with Native Americans. For example, in this shadowbox, you can see the bow and arrow, tomahawks and the large points constructed out of smaller points. From a scientific perspective, these displays are devoid of meaning because data tied to each artifact is missing. Today, the display serves instead to remind us about the ways in which history is written, and as this example shows, this can be done with artifacts and visual materials as well as paper and ink. *Courtesy of the New Haven Museum. Photograph by Jessica Zielonka.*

Opposite, bottom: Billy club and fireman's helmet. The traditions, rituals and objects developed around local police and fire services are, like the military branches, illuminating illustrations of the shaping of subcultures. New Haven's first full-time fire department was organized in 1862, although volunteer firemen had been in existence since Roger Sherman's organization of the first formal volunteer company in 1789. According to *The History of the New Haven Police Department*, published in 1892, the city's police department graduated from the status of "watchmen" into a formal organization to address the "frequent collisions of students and 'townies'…and the almost inevitable conflict whenever a fire broke out caused by the intense rivalry of the various fire companies." *Courtesy of the Connecticut Irish American Historical Society (billy club) and the New Haven Museum (helmet). Photograph by Jessica Zielonka.*

Next page: Indenture certificate for John Madigan, November 5, 1876. Indenture certificates spelled out the terms of service and were legal documents with official red wax stamps and the signatures of all involved, including witnesses. Madigan was placed into an apprenticeship service for a period of four years with John Moore, a harness maker. The certificate specified that Madigan "faithfully shall serve, his [master's] secrets shall keep, his lawful Commandments everywhere gladly do," and further, that he was not allowed to "play at cards, dice, tables" and that he could not "use or haunt taverns." The certificate was printed in Limerick, Ireland, and the challenging economic status of the Madigan family is apparent. Bridget Madigan, John's mother, gave her consent by signing next to her name with an "x." Madigan's indenture served him well—he became a harness maker in New Haven and was granted citizenship on October 25, 1884. *Courtesy of the Connecticut Irish American Historical Society. Photograph by Jessica Zielonka.*

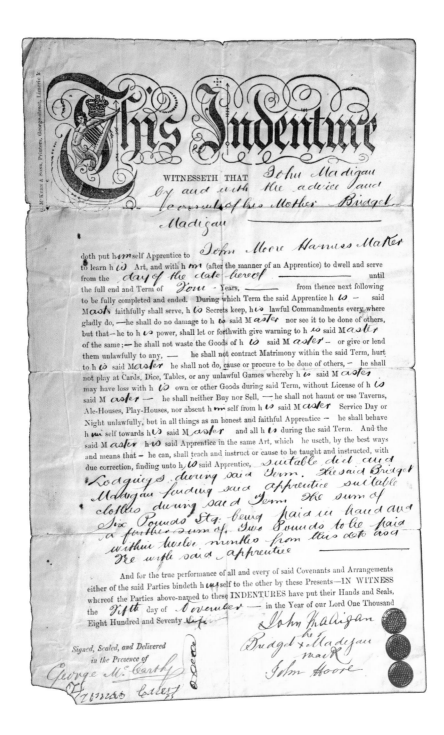

Father Michael McGiveny's cassock and diary, 1977.001.0045. This utilitarian date book kept appointments and notes for Father McGivney in 1879. The date book is inscribed, "M.J. McGivney/Christmas 1878" and, in another place, "from Mrs. Fagan, Whitney Ave." The date book records McGivney's busy days, with dates for special masses, visits for communion, "Last Rites" visits and funeral dates, as well as cash accounting notations. In just a few years, McGivney had built support for the fraternal lay organization called the Knights of Columbus, which held its first meeting in the basement of St. Mary's Church in New Haven on October 2, 1881. *Courtesy of the Knights of Columbus Museum, cassock photo by Jessica Zielonka, diary photo by the Knights of Columbus Museum.*

Next page, top: Baking tools used by Marzullo's Pastry Shop and mandolin, Amendola brothers, New Haven, circa 1920, 4600.2006. These objects speak to the early twentieth-century Italian Americans who lived in the Wooster Square neighborhood. Marzullo's opened in 1907 and eventually moved to Grand Avenue, while the Amendola brothers had a "Music Emporium" at 164 Wooster Street that became a neighborhood space for singing on Sunday mornings. *Baking tools courtesy of the Italian American Historical Society, photograph by Robert Velez; mandolin courtesy of Yale University Collection of Musical Instruments.*

Below: "Catalpa Jim" bust and Reynolds' Day ribbon. The story of the Catalpa is a unique testament to the close relations between New Haven Irish and the struggle for independence in nineteenth-century Ireland. James Reynolds, a brass molding foreman at the Sargent Company, played a critical role in the freeing of six Irishmen convicted for "Fenian" (Irish Republican) activities. Reynolds was a leader in the Clan Na Gael, the American organization that succeeded the earlier Fenian Brotherhood. Reynolds later owned his own brass foundry, first on Orange Street and then on East Street. *Courtesy of the Connecticut Irish American Historical Society. Photograph by Jessica Zielonka.*

PART V

EARLY TWENTIETH-CENTURY NEW HAVEN CELEBRATIONS

The first half of the twentieth century continued the tradition of significant celebrations, both for anniversaries with deeply historical flavor (and to mark the conclusion of World War I), and in the vein begun in the nineteenth century, to reinforce New Haven's enthusiasm for the ideals of "progress," specifically in the realm of commercial enterprise and civic projects. Smaller celebrations, commemorations and dedications were held throughout the first half of the twentieth century, including New Haven Irish societies marking "Reynolds' Day" in 1905; the memorial flagpole in Beecher Park on June 22, 1918; the installation of new monuments such as the Bennett Memorial Fountain on the Green in 1907; and a Labor Day parade held on September 4, 1939, marking the first statewide labor parade in New Haven for twenty-five years.

On November 11, 1918, when New Haven learned of the signing of the armistice, the *New Haven Evening Register* reported spontaneous celebrations breaking out all over the city, with sailors performing a "snake dance up and down the stretch from George Street to City Hall," while the Italians in the Wooster Square neighborhood "brought out their bands and the demonstrations approached the riotous." There were parades emanating from many of the city's factories, including Winchester, Marlina and Strouse-Adler, with many people carrying signs such as "The Kaiser's In the Soup!" and "The 102nd Will Soon Be Back!" Mayor David Fitzgerald immediately requested that New Haven "fly victory flags," and for "those engaged in the sale of spirits and intoxicating liquor...refrain from selling or dispensing such liquor during this 11th day of November, 1918." New Haven's Italian societies were at the heart of the celebrations because they had already been planning a celebration for Italy's victory over Austria and therefore had fireworks at the ready.

A formal celebration was set for the Green for Saturday, November 16, 1918, reported later as a "monster parade" in which "every eye was twinkling with joy." Multiple representations of the Kaiser were featured in the parade, including an effigy of the German leader sitting in an electric chair ("with the juices evidently turned on") that was prepared by one of the city's industrial societies. A baby pig wore a sign that read, "Here is the Kaiser tied to a chain in a pig pen." For the first time in a New Haven celebration, the use of confetti was part of the festivities, with the *Register* reporting the day after that "the Green this morning presented something of the appearance of a snow storm, being completely littered with confetti and refuse paper of every description." The appearance of confetti got a mention in multiple articles because "the vendors ran out and started selling it by the handful."

Also of note during the first half of the twentieth century was the Connecticut tercentenary, celebrated in 1935. Events were planned both at the state and local level, and in New Haven, the New Haven Colony Historical

Peace celebration souvenir program, November 16, 1918. *Courtesy of the Connecticut Irish American Historical Society.*

Society took the lead, holding a meeting on May 23, 1934, to discuss the city's participation in the celebration. This resulted in New Haven holding a variety of events over the course of the summer and fall, including a concert at Yale Bowl, a track and field meet, a reenactment of the British invasion of New Haven and the State Tercentenary Military Ball, which was preceded by a dinner sponsored by the New Haven Tercentenary Committee. The state tercentenary gave form to New Haven's own tercentenary three years later, producing a stamp, a medal and a fifty-cent piece. Much of this work was done with the sponsorship of the Works Progress Administration federal relief programs, and the subcommittee for the medal was headed by Bancel LaFarge, a muralist who lived in Hamden.

POWDER HOUSE DAY, APRIL 1905

Once more, I demand the keys.
—reenactment speech for Benedict Arnold

Though a recent article in the *Branford Patch* suggested that New Haven has celebrated Powder House Day for 237 years, the celebration was actually an invention of the early twentieth century, not surprisingly by a member of the Second Company Governor's Foot Guard. New Haven's oldest militia company, the Second Company was formed by an ambitious Benedict Arnold in late 1774 following the creation of the First Company in Hartford in 1771 (both cities were the co-capitals at the time). Aaron Burr, Ethan Allen and James Hillhouse were among the first members. While members of the Second Company usually participated in New Haven celebrations, the development of the reenactment of Powder House Day was a product of the period after the American centennial in 1876 that prompted the colonial revival in American culture. Locally, there was a great interest in New Haven's colonial history, manifested in celebrations (Centennial of Evacuation of New Haven, 1879), monument building (Defender's Square Memorial, 1911) and architecture (Union and New Haven Trust Company building, 205 Church Street, 1927) that lasted well into the twentieth century. Thus, it is not a surprise that the Second Company would look back at its own central role in Revolutionary events and revive an event already dramatic in its original form with the

Powder House Day, New Haven, April 2012 reenactment and parade march. *Photograph by Laura A. Macaluso.*

"blazing red color of the full dress uniform with bearskin hats," as the *Register* reported in 1975.

Powder House Day was created by the Second Company Governor's Foot Guard chaplain Watson L. Phillips and was first celebrated on April 24, 1905, on the 130th anniversary of the event. The first reenactment was clearly a success, and at the banquet following the activities, members of the company noted that they usually celebrated their anniversary on March 2 with a banquet and then held a separate church service on a different day. At once, the members voted to combine the two events into one annual Foot Guard day every April 24. New Haven participated fully, and "the city was in holiday dress in honor of the 'The Feeters.'" The First Company Governor's Foot Guard from Hartford traveled by special train to take part, gaining special mention in the newspaper, which reported that the "Hartford Footers won fresh laurels here today." The Second Company met the First at Union Station, and together they marched to the armory and then to the Church of the Redeemer for a commemorative service. The purpose of the church visit was to remember members who had passed the year before with an elaborate ceremony of memorial hymn, the reading of scriptures, a reading of the "necrological roll" (taps was played when the names were read) and more music, including "The Star-Spangled Banner" and "Fling Out the Banner, Let It Wave." After the ceremony, the Feeters gathered together and marched to city hall, traveling via Orange Street to Trumbull, Whitney, Sachem, Hillhouse, Grove Street and College and then to Elm, York, Chapel and finally Church Street.

Eventually, the Powder House Day reenactment was codified into a script, the essence of which is still used today. The focus of the reenactment is Captain Benedict Arnold and Lieutenant Leavenworth, represented by the major commandant of the Second Company and his adjutant; Colonel Wooster, represented by a member of one of New Haven's patriotic societies; and selectmen, represented by the mayor of New Haven and other city officials. It was a fine moment for Arnold, building a reputation that would be burnished during the strategically important Revolutionary War battle of Saratoga. The words spoken during the 1905 reenactment were certainly more verbose than what is overheard today on Powder House Day. In 1905, the reenactors used city hall as the stage set, just as they do today, reciting:

Mr. Selectman: "Major Weed, commandant of the Governor's Foot Guard, which command stands aligned in front of this building en route to Lexington, requests that you deliver to him the keys to the powder house that he may supply his men with ammunition."

"Who is this Major Weed that makes this demand on the selectmen?"

"I have already told you he is commandant of the Second Company, Governor's Foot Guard, now on their march to Lexington, and he is not to be trifled with or delayed; further, he is 'first in war, first in peace and first in the hearts of his command.'"

"The selectmen will take time to consider this demand before entirely ignoring the authority of the king."

"Major Weed, who cares nothing about your old king, anticipating your possible refusal, demands the keys to the powder house, and unless you deliver them to him, in five minutes, he will order the company to break it open and furnish themselves."

"Well, here are the keys. We suppose we might as well submit to this order, under protest, however, with loyalty to the king."

After this first reenactment, the Second Company marched around the Green, entering by the North Gate for review by Governor Roberts and his staff.

The Naval Militia set off a thirteen-gun salute, and a dress parade followed. The "Star-Spangled Banner" was played, while the flag on the liberty pole on the Green was lowered. Finally, everyone headed to Harmonie Hall for a banquet. At the banquet, a series of toasts was given, including to the State of Connecticut, to the City of New Haven, to Yale and the American wars and to the Foot Guard in the Revolution, as well as "Greetings to the First Company." Afterward, the Second Company escorted the First Company back to the train station. Powder House Day made the local news for many years afterward, demonstrating continued interest in the event. In 1907, the banquet was held at the Tontine Hotel, but by 1913, after the Tontine was demolished, the Taft had become the banquet hall of choice. The *Saturday Chronicle* (New Haven edition) of April 19, 1913, reported that Benjamin Jepson, a captain the Foot Guard and New Haven's famed music teacher, had been participating in events since before the Civil War. He was still here in 1913. William H. Taft, one-term president and now professor at Yale University, was given honorary membership in the Foot Guard, and he was scheduled to "felicitate with the Feeters" before the event. Not surprisingly, the largest attendance to witness Powder House Day happened in 1938, when New Haven was resplendently decorated for the tercentenary.

The years leading up to the American bicentennial in 1976 saw the revitalization of Powder House Day. In 1974, the Green received National Historic Landmark status, and a bronze plaque stating such was placed on the Green during Powder House Day. This was the first of two weekends intended to kick off the American bicentennial year. Two thousand people attended. At the 1975 Powder House Day, the *Register* noted that the crowd booed at the appropriate moment (when the city councilmen refuse to turn over the keys). Then, on May 25, 1975, a Powder House Ball was held at the New Haven Lawn Club, with attendees in costume. Called a "warm-up for the Bicentennial" by the *New Haven Register*, the decorations included mannequins dressed as a drummer boy, Betsy Ross and the Indian girl Shaumishuh (Sachem Momauguin's sister), among others. Mrs. John Hill was the organizer, and to raise money for the New Haven Bicentennial Commission, the ball featured a "Historical Hysterical Auction" that resulted in $600. A champagne breakfast followed at midnight. The mood was pure 1776/1976 as guests danced "under an array of colorful Colonial flags" and six hundred helium balloons. In 1988, at New Haven's 350th anniversary, the New Haven Colony Historical Society also held a Powder House Day Brawl party that was actually a dance—the word "brawl" being a derivative from the French *braule*, meaning a dance that has gotten out of control.

New Haven Week, September 1912

Old Elms, New Ideas—New Haven.
—official program, New Haven Week Celebration

The first major event of the twentieth century was New Haven Week, held September 19–21, 1912. In addition to the ephemera produced for New Haven Week, the availability of photography to the masses begins to provide ever more documentation of New Haven's celebrations where once lengthy newspaper reports were the only descriptors. The New Haven Chamber of Commerce, which had first made its appearance in celebrations in the second half of the nineteenth century, was now the sponsor of major events. Under the slogan "Old Elms, New Ideas—New Haven," the chamber of commerce desired a "co-operative, open-hearted commonwealth in which business and education are main cogs in the wheel of progress, [which] enters a new day of expansion." Called "enterprising and aggressive" by Mayor Frank J. Rice, the chamber of commerce wanted a "great awakening for the old 'City of Elms'" and foresaw a "celebration of this kind, which will be followed by even bigger ones in the future."

New Haven Week program. *Courtesy of the Jewish Historical of Greater New Haven. Photograph by Jessica Zielonka.*

Mayor Rice, whose photograph is labeled "New Haven's Progressive Chief Executive" in the souvenir program, presented his belief that "New Haven Week gives us a horizon to bound our present growth, and to survey our almost limitless outlook for the future." He was not pleased that visitors to New Haven would see only a fraction of his progressive plans for the city during the three-day event. Clearly, he and the chamber of commerce were of the same mind—not surprising since Rice was a businessman himself (as were all of New Haven mayors from the mid-nineteenth century onward). The scope of his dream for New Haven, and likely the dream of his colleagues in the chamber, was summarized in the souvenir program as

a water-front like those of the Old World, stretching for miles along a deepened harbor channel, fringed by a spacious driveway and dotted by parks; streets laid with the most durable of permanent pavements; playgrounds created and maintained zealously in the congested city districts, the finest Union Depot approach in New England, transferring from the largest railroad station between Boston and New York with facility and dispatch shoppers and visitors to the business center and residential districts; and a grand new municipal group of structures—these are some of the external transformations of the immediate future.

In 1910, the City of New Haven had hired urban planners and architects Cass Gilbert and Frederick Law Olmsted Jr. to produce a plan for the Elm City. Most of the plan never came to fruition, but in 1912, the plan would not have been shelved yet for the next new idea, and the fervent spirit in which they worked was clear.

The New Haven Chamber of Commerce included all the standard ingredients in its celebration of New Haven, including music, a military parade, "artistically decorated vehicles" (modernized, sanitized versions

New Haven Week pennant. *Courtesy of Joseph Taylor. Photograph by Jessica Zielonka.*

"Court of Honor" at New Haven Week, photograph, September 1912. *Courtesy of Joseph Taylor.*

of carriage-bound antiques and horribles) and historical floats. The New Haven Week parade was the first time that a number of prizes were awarded, though it is difficult to imagine that prizes were not given out in earlier years. The largest prize offered was $200 for the best industrial float.

Not to be outdone by any previous celebration in New Haven, the chamber of commerce designed a fireworks program over three days and nights that was centered on the story of "The Last Days of Pompeii," which sounds like an excuse to set off massive amounts of fireworks with names like Aladdin's Jeweled Tree and new Neapolitan bombshells. This event marks the first time that daylight fireworks were part of any celebration in New Haven and, as far as I know, the last time as well. The final Saturday evening event of the week featured 115 different types of fireworks. Evidently, the fireworks displays that we see today, whether in New Haven or in other New England cities, are pitiable in comparison. Finally, a triumphal archway was constructed, most likely out of wood and plaster, through which the formal procession passed. Quickly constructed structures were a feature of the 1892 World's Columbian Exposition in Chicago (the so-called White City), and New Haven Week repeated the idea with its own court of honor, although on a much smaller scale. The success of New Haven Week prompted the chamber of commerce to sponsor more events, such as the New Haven Progress Exhibition in 1926–27.

NEW HAVEN TERCENTENARY, APRIL 1938

They took the elm and the iron, the heat and the killing frost,
And from them they built the city, and we live in it today.
—from "The Tercentenary Ode," Stephen Vincent Benét, 1938

As we have seen, there were many celebrations in New Haven before the tercentenary in 1938 and some that followed it, but this event remains firmly fixed as the climax of all city birthday celebrations, surpassing others in terms of length, number of activities, cooperation between city and university and the use of merchandising and marketing. That this remarkable celebration happened in the midst of the Great Depression and European troubles was determined by several factors, most importantly a beloved Irish American mayor and the availability of funds from the Roosevelt administration's Works Progress Administration program.

Incongruous as it seems today, on April 25, 1938, the 300th anniversary of the founding of New Haven, the headline of the *New Haven Journal Courier* was "Nazi Minority Threatens Czechs." Centered directly under that bold, black headline is a photograph of New Haveners filing into Center Church, with the caption, "Obeying the imperative church call sounded by the snare drummer." The photograph featured a man dressed in Pilgrim hat, waistcoat and breeches and beating a borrowed drum made in 1829. A sign placed in front of Center Church read, "After the manner of the Puritans," which apparently included "four brightly uniformed sentries" stationed in front of Center Church who "guarded against Indian attacks." Meanwhile, the front page of the *Courier* also had "Archbishop Arrested in Soviet Purge" and "Poles Are Aroused as Czechs Fire on Balloon," which should lead us to ask what New Haven was hoping to accomplish by putting on such a show in this uncertain time.

The year before, Mayor John W. Murphy had appointed Judge John L. Gilson chairman of the committee to arrange for the celebration of the New Haven's tercentenary. A general committee of twenty-five was formed, and from there subcommittees were formed. The festival committee, headed by Gilson, designed the events held at the Yale Bowl, while a professional firm from New York, Gerome H. Cargill, was hired to design the Industrial Exposition and historical pageant. A third committee was charged with handling all of the other events. In the end, close to three hundred volunteer planning committee members were involved, giving shape to the extravaganza.

Tercentenary plaque. *Courtesy of Joseph Taylor. Photograph by Jessica Zielonka.*

This included the expected (the festival committee, publicity committee and finance committee) but also the unexpected (the committee on horseshoes, with three members; the committee on skeet shooting; and, signaling New Haven's large Italian American community, the committee on bocce). For the first time during New Haven celebrations, women had their own committee, in addition to there being several sports committees for women, including golf, tennis and a committee on "scoutcraft" for girls. The multiple moving parts of the tercentenary celebration veered from the sacred to the profane, from cherished relics to mass-produced souvenirs. The event was spread out over almost two months and was also spread out over the city.

The tercentenary began at sundown (6:39 p.m.) on Friday, April 23, 1938 with many New Haven Jews attending synagogue—the first time that a

Tercentenary tray. *Courtesy of Joseph Taylor. Photograph by Jessica Zielonka.*

minority ethnic group in New Haven "led" an anniversary celebration in the city. On Sunday, a Colonial Service was held at Woolsey Hall at 8:00 p.m., led by Dr. Oscar Maurer, the fourteenth rector of Center Church. The crowd was expected to be outsized, and thus the religious subcommittee debated whether to put speakers on the exterior façade of Woolsey so the crowd could listen, but the idea was nixed when it was determined that other church services going on at the same time would suffer. One of the nods to the past, as reported by the *New Haven Journal-Courier*, was the inclusion of "tythingmen" who "will pace the aisles, their tip-staves ready to prod mischievous children or to tickle the chins of dozing adults," as well as an hourglass to "record the passing of time as the minister preaches on 'The Enduring Values of the Puritan Faith.'" Striving to re-create a sense of seventeenth-century religious life in New Haven, the organ was banished. The hour-long oration was noted as being two hours shorter than John Davenport's sermon under the oak. One of the invited speakers was Governor Wilbur Cross, who was reported as saying, "America today as a people have fallen far away from the great traditions of the Puritans," but he added that a "'comeback' was not too much to hope for in New Haven." This sentiment expresses a yearning for a return to the values of the past, but this would always be in conflict with progress and its value system (as exemplified in New Haven Week). Governor Cross said as much, stating, "Even in Colonial times, the problem was not all Indians, but the application of morals and economics."

The use of Native American people and heritage was, once again, both denigrating and false, built on a century of narrative that had both written New England natives out of existence and appropriated incorrect ideas into white culture. For example, after the tercentenary's historical pageant, the May 29 edition of the *New Haven Register* reported, "Indians a Standout. For sheer color, the groups of Indians in the procession were head and shoulders above everything else." Just as in earlier nineteenth-century celebrations, these were white men from the social clubs called Hammonasset, Tribe No. 1, and the Order of the Red Man, as well as other "tribes" from around the state such as Narkeeta Council 27, Degree of Pocahontas. The *Register* also reported pleasure in seeing "another bower-enveloped truck carrying a genuine tepee and brightly painted Indians in scarlet and blue feathers." One of the official souvenir/marketing items was a postcard showing a group of men sitting on the Green and sending smoke signals. Native

Postcard: "Symbolizing the Indian custom of sending messages by means of smoke signals, this group gathered on the central Green was smoke signals of welcome were sent forth inviting all absent friends of New Haven to join in the 300th Anniversary of its founding. Greeting—we want you to be sure to come to New Haven for at least one or two of the many interesting events to be held during our 300th Birthday Celebration." *Courtesy of the Whitney Library, New Haven Museum, MSS #B-3, Box 17, Folder D.*

Americans from New Haven or any other Connecticut town were not part of the tercentenary beyond these representations. The historical pageant, the highlight of the Tercentenary Festival, featured the "Indian Village" as the first scene, with no fewer than one hundred New Haveners playing "Indian Men and Women." Four men were also "Tom Tom Players." One participant and viewer of the pageant wrote in her notes about "the business of gleeful excitement over mirrors, etc."

The next event, Powder House Day, was held on Monday, April 26. The Second Company Governor's Foot Guard was now an expected participant in New Haven celebrations (and the dates also fit easily as the anniversary of Powder House Day is April 21). At 1:00 p.m., there was a luncheon for guests of the Second Company, then at 2:30 p.m., the company marched from the armory to Center Church via Broadway, Elm, Temple and Church Streets, where a brief service was given. At 5:00 p.m., Powder House Day was reenacted, with a thirteen-gun salute and a reception at Union League, followed by dinner at the Taft Hotel.

The next tercentenary events happened in May, including the presentation of a giant birthday cake on the lower Green by schoolchildren on May 18, paid for by a penny-march. The next day, the Tercentenary Festival opened, and on May 21, Mayor Murphy sent messengers on horseback from the Horse Guard to all the neighboring towns, many once part of the New Haven Colony, inviting their participation in the upcoming parade on May 28. The original colony towns of Branford, Guilford, Stamford, Milford and Southold, Long Island, all marked the occasion with church services in their own towns, and on May 29, a Community Praise and Memorial Service was held at the Yale Bowl, where Governor Wilbur Cross was the main speaker.

On June 5, a "School Day" was held, for which all public schools closed at 11:00 a.m. so that schoolchildren could see the events, and on June 6, "State Day," Stephen Vincent Benét read "The Tercentenary Ode" the night before *Through Many Generations: A Pageant of Historic New Haven* opened at the Yale Bowl. Benét was a Stonington, Connecticut resident and member of the Yale class of 1919. He had won the Pulitzer Prize ten years earlier for his epic poem "John Brown's Body," and two years before the New Haven tercentenary, he wrote the short story "The Devil and Daniel Webster," which won the O. Henry Award and was made into a 1941 RKO film starring Walter Huston as Old Scratch (Benét contributed to the screenplay). In the midst of a busy career, Benét took the time to pen the following poem, and he also read it in New Haven:

Tercentenary birthday cake image from the New Haven tercentenary, with inscription on back, "Center Church Steeple in the background, the flagpole at the right." *Courtesy of the Whitney Library, New Haven Museum, MSS #B-3, Box 17, Folder C.*

"The Tercentenary Ode"

They came, in showery April, to the sweet, cold shore, and the rocks,
The exiles, sure of their purpose, but not yet one with the land,
And they saw it, gracious and goodly, but savage as deer or fox.
But beyond it they saw a city that was not built by the hand.
Davenport, Eaton, Turner, they planted their nine-square town.
The new fire burned on the hearthstone, the houses fronted the day
And yet it was small and lonely, when the first deep snows came down.
It was then they remembered England and all they had cast away.
The known street, the known neighbor, the graves where kinfolk lie.
The settled life, the sure ending, the thousand small, clutching things.
What were they doing here, under naked and endless sky,
Where the wolf ran wild in the forest by the lodges of the forest-kings?
They did not question the purpose. They did not cry "We are lost
For we do not walk as our fathers and this is a bitter way."

They took the elm and the iron, the heat and the killing frost.
And from them they built the city, and we live in it today.
The Fall with his sachem colors, the Summer wind by the shore.
The Spring like an Indian runner, beautiful, stripped and swift.
They knew these things in their season—and yet there was something more.
And they thought not only of harvest when they thanked their God for his gift.
Zealot, rebel, dissenter—there was something they wished to build.
A secret, a shining city, more great than the years outworn,
And they died at the end of labor, the vision yet unfulfilled,
But the land cleared and the town made and the strong children born.
Rigid and sure of Zion—they were that—and we know it well.
The exile oppressed the exiled, the righteous harried the just
And the souls of the unredeemed were brush for the fires of hell
It is not for that we purpose we praise them, though they would think that
  we must.
Not that but views of iron that lasted the winter out.
The women, who longed for England and died on the stool of birth.
The moral courage, and failure, the mortal patience and doubt
And the vision of something greater not yet built on the earth.
It has flickered and changed and altered with time and the changing years,
But we know this much of their vision, we know this much in our day,
Had they known but fear of the outcome, they would have died with their fears,
But they built as they lived, strong-handed and the work has not passed away.
Regicide, merchant, scholar—exile of every stock,
All those who shared in the labor, all those who opened the ways
And left us the growing lilac and the fire within the rock.
The men who were not contented, the men that their children praise.

"The Tercentenary Ode" set the tone for the *Pageant of Historic New Haven*, which Mayor John Murphy praised afterward, stating, "Too long had this city deferred telling the story of its birth and development in the way it has just been told." Not surprisingly, George Dudley Seymour, New Haven's colonial revival authority, proposed the scenes for the historical pageant, which was produced professionally under the direction of William F. Marlatt. About 3,500 people took part, in addition to live oxen and cows and antique carriages. The seats cost twenty-five cents. In twenty-two "stirring scenes," narrator (and Yale professor of public speaking) Hubert Graves recounted New Haven legends such as "The Phantom Ship," "The Regicides" and a "gay ball scene performing the stately dancing of the late 19th century."

"Yale boys" participated in "The Gay Nineties" episodes. The narration was written by Bernard Victory Dryer, whose typed notes survive in the Whitney Library. Toward the end of his synopsis of the pageant, Dryer wrote, "a paragraph was inserted here shortly before the pageant opened, describing two or three of the outstanding inventions of the period; all of them were invented by New Haveners. One was the invention of the vulcanized rubber process, another had to do with the telephones; what the third one was, I can't recall." You can almost hear Dryer's disinterest in manufacturing life. In fact, in the pageant there are no scenes taking place in factories or stores, only a "Firemen's Picnic" and an "Automobile Party." The tercentenary did have a subcommittee on industrial history, but it had only three members.

If the Tercentenary Festival and pageant were dedicated to early New Haven history sans industrial history, the other side of New Haven identity was celebrated at the Progress Exposition, held at Coxe Field House, where local business firms and manufacturing industries presented displays. As advertised, "See Television—most startling advancement of modern times," was displayed along with Eli Whitney's cotton gin, as well as many examples of "modern machinery making world famous products…and many more rare and unusual sights." The culture of television was already making an impact on the landscape, with a "Television City" where New Haveners such as Barbara Kent Hickey experienced television—some for the first time, although Hickey penciled in her notes from the event, "television is still terribly crude."

In terms of exhibits, it wasn't all song and dance. New Haven history was on display during the tercentenary in several locations. Visitors saw historic objects at Sterling Memorial Library, which put on "a most unusual exhibit of historic documents—maps, manuscripts, prints, books and broadsides, contributed by the City of New Haven, Center and United Churches." The New Haven Colony Historical Society also offered an exhibit of more colonial artifacts, many on loan (likely from board members and friends), in the ballroom of the Pardee-Morris House from May 25 through June 15. The New Haven Public Library displayed paintings formerly owned by William Scranton Pardee from May 10 to June 22 and again from October 1 to October 15. For the first time in New Haven, signs were erected around town to mark historic sites. Designed in the form of a shield with the inscription "1638/1938," you can see one of these shields on the Green, circa 1938, in the photograph at the front of this book that accompanies the song "The Birth of New-Haven." The history committee may have also contributed to the production of the tercentennial medallion. Strangely,

New Haven tercentenary medal, Julio Kilenyi, silver, 32mm, 1938, 2001.87.26488. *Courtesy of the Yale University Art Gallery, transfer from Sterling Memorial Library, Yale University.*

George Dudley Seymour did not serve on this committee. If he had, it would be hard to imagine that he would have agreed to reproducing Hezekiah Auger's 1838 medal as the official medallion. The reuse speaks highly to the continuing influence of Auger's design, but the 1938 reproduction is very poor and does nothing to capture the spirit of *their* age.

As with earlier New Haven celebrations, the planning committee wanted to mark the landscape with monuments and memorials that would outlast the event itself. Two stone memorials were erected during the tercentennial, one a cenotaph to Theophilus Eaton on the exterior of Center Church and the other a tablet in the southeast corner of Center Church, marking the location of the first meetinghouse. In addition, feeling a little more charitable toward John Davenport this time around (as opposed to the Founders' Day planning committee), a wreath was sent to Boston to be laid on Davenport's grave in the King's Chapel Burial Ground. A huge wreath was also hung over the bronze plaque placed on the building at the corner of College and Elm; the plaque was installed by the Founders' Day planning committee in 1888 to mark the location of Davenport's sermon under the oak.

Like earlier celebrations, the records of the tercentenary committee tell us this event wrapped up with a balance of $8,857.20, which was given to the New Haven Colony Historical Society. The state had provided the city a contribution of $21,315.00, to which $8,338.00 was raised by New Haveners and another $1,971.33 from sales of souvenirs, ball tickets, rental space, exhibits, pageant tickets and the children's penny-march. If Mayor John Murphy had anything to do with the finances of the tercentenary committee, this makes sense. Through austerity measures and advocating on behalf of New Haven with the federal government for loans and work relief programs, by 1933 Murphy was able to balance the city's budget and, by 1938, fully restore city employee salaries. Marketed as the "event of a lifetime," the tercentenary saw a parade in which 20,000 people marched, witnessed by 150,000 people, and four hundred messages were sent from around the globe to Center Church "expressing friendliness and goodwill." The tercentenary was called "epoch making," and though the last night of the pageant was washed out by rain, overall it was deemed the "Best in the History of the City."

In New Haven, the last large celebratory events of the first half of the twentieth century were V-E Day and V-J Day, marking the end of World War II. President Harry Truman announced the unconditional surrender of Germany at 9:00 a.m. on May 8, 1945. But instead of the instantaneous celebrations that were seen at the end of World War I, according to the *New Haven Evening Register*, "the city's first reaction to the successful ending of the war in Europe was tempered with the solemnity of respect for those who died in making the victory possible and the fact that a costly war with Japan is still ahead." It was reported that munitions workers at Winchester and High Standard "shut down for the day" and that "most stores and all bars, grills and package stores closed." "This may or may not be V-E Day," noted the *Register*, but "New Haven is generally marking the day as such." Under direction from President Truman, prayer services for "unfinished tasks" at noon and in the evening hours were held at many churches and synagogues.

This was very different from the around-the-clock celebrations held in New York City, where 500,000 people jammed into Times Square amid a "hailstorm of torn telephone books, colored rags, streamers and confetti." In New Haven, the police and fire departments were at the ready, but the only disturbance reported by the *Register* was a group of boys from City Point that "paraded around the neighborhood whooping it up, and then hanged Hitler in effigy." Even the city's downtown stores, which had been under "brownout" regulations, did not illuminate their windows. Adding to the "quiet feelings and sincere expressions of thanks," the flagpole on the Green was hanging at half-staff due to the death of Franklin Delano Roosevelt on April 12. Two days later, a concession to celebrating in New Haven came in the form of an outsized American flag hung by Osterweis and Sons at 20 Church Street. The flag was thirty-six by eighteen feet and apparently "covered four of the five floors of the building and shut off considerable light from the workrooms." Malley's, too, had a special illuminated display of Uncle Sam surrounded by flags.

But all this would be little compared to the unleashing of emotion in just three months' time when New Haven would "Whoop It Up in Riotous Fashion" when the Japanese surrendered on August 14, 1945. The news of surrender was heard at 4:00 a.m., and immediately the "City [Gave Itself] Over to Victory Celebration." More than sixty bonfires were lit around the city, auto horns were blown and cars were decorated with bunting, while still others "dragged tin cans and other noise-markers behind." One man in Fair Haven shot off his pistol, the *Register* reported. Rolls of paper were flung over telephone wires, giving the Wooster Square area a "holiday appearance." August 14 and 15 were eventually declared national holidays by President Truman. New Haven celebrated but kept close the "Gold Stars and leaden hearts" that represented almost five hundred men from the Elm City killed during the course of the war.

TREASURES FROM EARLY TWENTIETH-CENTURY NEW HAVEN

The early twentieth century is a potent moment to observe the creation of Yale University's image, still firmly in place today and recycled every year when freshmen arrive and seniors graduate or when a varsity game is played. A convergence of song, architecture, athletic traditions and even choice of school color contributed to shaping an image for the university. With Yale's own bicentennial in 1901 and another huge bicentennial event in 1916 (marking the anniversary of the university's move from Saybrook to New Haven), the objects and images from this period in Yale history speak to a renewed dedication to a culture and tradition that today seems timeless. However, they are man-made creations, still evolving in the twenty-first century with the addition of two new residential colleges and the advent of Open Yale Courses, which offer introductory Yale University courses for free to anyone with an Internet connection.

Opposite: Rah! Rah! Rah! Thomas Royal White, circa 1900, 1996.13.3. Yale blue is much in evidence in this watercolor from the turn of the twentieth century, showing how quickly the color became a signature for the university—green was the school color until 1894, when the university followed the crew team, which had rowed in blue since the 1850s. The popularity of rowing is seen in the other objects grouped here—the hat pin in the shape of an oar, which could have been worn by the cheering woman with Gibson girl figure, and the interior of Mory's, which has oars inscribed with the dates of Ivy League rowing competitions hanging from the ceilings. *Courtesy of the New Haven Museum, gift of Frank Perri. Photograph by Jessica Zielonka.*

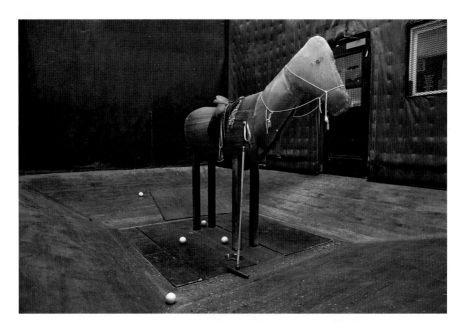

Wooden horse for polo practice. The wooden practice horse for the polo club is still in use, likely installed in Payne Whitney Gymnasium soon after its completion in 1932. Built of wooden slats nailed onto a form, students have drawn eyes on the canvas bag that serves as the head. The four sides to the room are at a high angle, forcing the ball to bounce swiftly from different angles. *Courtesy of the Yale Athletic Department, Yale University. Photograph by Jessica Zielonka.*

Opposite, top: *Bulldog!* Songbook cover, Cole Porter, published by Chas. F. Smith, 1105 Chapel Street, New Haven, Connecticut. Handsome Dan, the first official mascot in collegiate history, was purchased for five dollars from a New Haven blacksmith in 1889. It's hard to deny the winning team of Handsome Dan and Cole Porter, a Yale student who found great success on Broadway in the 1930s. "Bull-dog! Bull-dog! Bow wow wow, Our team can never fail. When the sons of Eli break through the line, That is the sign we hail." *Courtesy of the Irving S. Gilmore Music Library, Yale University.*

Opposite, bottom: Original Old Campus fence for Yale captain's photographs. Original sections of the Old Campus fence at Yale exist in several places, including Sterling Memorial Library and this part, used since the late nineteenth century for all Yale University captain's photographs, many of which are on display at Mory's. New Haven's famous elm trees, painted in gray tones, provide the backdrop. The original fence, a demarcation between Yale and the city, was one of the most important locations for male students to hang out and enjoy the passing of urban life. *Courtesy of Yale University Athletics, Ray Tompkins House, Yale University. Photograph by Jessica Zielonka.*

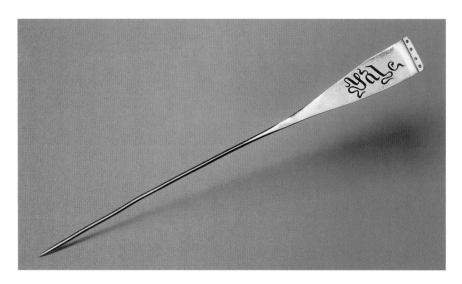

Hat pin in the shape of an oar, 1897, sterling silver, gold and blue enamel, 15.081cm x 1.27cm, 2006. 2009.181.6. *Courtesy of the Yale University Art Gallery, gift of Graham C. Boettcher, BA 1995, PhD.*

Table at Mory's with Whiffenpoofs carving. The Whiffenpoofs (or the "Whiffs") were the first collegiate a capella group, still performing at Mory's on Monday nights. Its song traces the history of the memorabilia-laden membership club: "To the tables down at Mory's, to the place where Louis dwells, To the dear old Temple Bar we love so well, Sing the Whiffenpoofs assembled with their glasses raised on high." *Courtesy of Mory's. Photograph by Jessica Zielonka.*

PART VI

LATE TWENTIETH-CENTURY NEW HAVEN CELEBRATIONS

E normous social changes of the late twentieth century, coupled with an exodus to the suburbs, led to the dissipation of many urban traditions but also the creation of others (or, in the case of New Haven's St. Patrick's Day Parade, the reinstitution of a tradition that had ended at the turn of the twentieth century). Membership in churches and social clubs waned, affecting the frequency and size of celebrations, but New Haven managed to produce two large-scale celebrations during the second half of the twentieth century, including leading the state in American bicentennial celebrations in 1976 and committing itself to another semi-centennial, this one for the city's 350th anniversary in 1988. The challenge, and it's one that still remains, is how to bridge two sensibilities—an interest and reuse of the past, with all of its shortcomings, and the views and desires of twenty-first-century pluralistic society.

AMERICAN BICENTENNIAL, JULY 1976

All of today's salutes will not be exploding for the Bicentennial.
                                        —Elm City Clarion, *July 4, 1976*

The bicentennial of the United States of America in 1976 was a great amalgamation of the historical reverberations that we have seen in earlier celebrations. Popular consumer culture was, by now, the dominant cultural force in American society. All one needs to do is think of actor Telly Savalas blowing kisses from an "antique" car in the parade in Washington, D.C., to realize that the 1976 event was the 1876 centennial all over again. It was expansive, brash and filled with fireworks—a surge of red, white and blue in an otherwise dreary, oil-deprived decade. A remark in the *New Haven Register* that "this is what we need after Watergate" suggests that the bicentennial served as a much-needed adrenaline boost for Americans. Even President Gerald Ford sanctioned the celebrations, saying, "Break out the flags, strike up the band, light up the sky…there are times for solemn ceremonies, but we Americans are uncomfortable with too much solemnity…this is the probably the only country that puts the 'pursuit of happiness' first."

Across the country and abroad, there were plenty of opportunities for celebration, with some activities that would have fit in very well with the "antiques and horribles" of the nineteenth century. The Associated Press reported that one family in Utah painted a "historical American flag on the bottom of their pool," while Lake City, Pennsylvania, built a landing pad for unidentified flying objects and ringed it with red, white and blue lights. A twenty-foot-long time capsule in Seward, Nebraska, was filled with ten thousand items, including a yellow Chevy Vega. *Ripley's Believe It or Not–*type activities ruled the day: Glenwood Springs, Colorado, made the world's largest pancake (seventy-six inches in diameter); Minneapolis held the world's largest ice cream social; Ontario, California, set the world's longest picnic table; Los Angeles held the longest bicentennial parade; Baltimore made the biggest birthday cake (sixty-nine thousand pounds); and the town of George, Washington, baked a gigantic cherry pie. There was a serious side, too, of course: the size of the pancake, birthday cake and pie were topped only by the ten thousand people who became naturalized American citizens on the Fourth of July 1976. Even Queen Elizabeth came to visit (her grandmother, Victoria, had not in 1876), although it was Douglas Fairbanks, American-born but knighted by the British empire, who read the Declaration of Independence from the steps of St. Paul's Cathedral in London. More than one hundred celebrations were held around the United Kingdom.

Many people complained about the commercialism and perceived trivial interests of the bicentennial celebrations (some called the event the "Buy-Centennial"). The *Register* reported one New Havener saying that "after 200 years the country is entitled to a celebration, but, I think part of the celebration should have been devoted to a lot more debate and discussion of the problems we face today." This, in fact, did happen in cities like New

Haven and elsewhere, but town hall–type meetings dedicated to discussion were overshadowed by fireworks. President Ford struck a different tone from his "pursuit of happiness" comment when in his bicentennial statement (President Ulysses S. Grant had done the same in 1876) he encouraged the "questioning, examination and criticism of society" because "the American adventure is a continuing process." If we ever doubted the long arm of history in our own twenty-first-century lives, seemingly far removed from the 1970s, we have only to read Ford's words:

> *Increasing independence and opportunity for all Americans, insurance of the right to privacy, the creation of a more beautiful and safer America and the promotion of a stable international order…there is a distrust of government. There is the realization today, just as there was when founding fathers drew up the Constitution, that government cannot give us personal fulfillment…Can we retain personal liberty in a world that more and more is threatened by terrorism, on a national and global scale? Will we have to submit to Big Brother surveillance, give up our privacy, to protect ourselves against criminals who are mobile and armed with modern weapons that make lawlessness an unacceptable danger?*

Terrorism, both domestic and international, was on Ford's mind. The New Haven newspaper headlines about the bicentennial shared space with stories about the Air France plane carrying 106 passengers that was hijacked by pro-Palestinian supporters, but terrorism was happening on American soil as well. Four bombs went off in Massachusetts and New Hampshire in the weeks leading up to the Fourth of July, one of which destroyed an Electra propjet plane at Logan International Airport and another a post office in the coastal town of Seabrook, New Hampshire. Thus, in addition to the sheer patriotic fervor, the bicentennial was an opportunity for numerous groups to utilize the event for attention, some menacing and others peaceful, including American neo-Nazis who attempted to march in Lafayette Park in Washington, D.C., across from the White House and a planned showdown between white supremacists in Kentucky and the police (thankfully washed away by rain). Native Americans also "demonstrated for the survival of the American Indian."

The premature start to planning the bicentennial demonstrates the importance that the event held for the country and in historic cities such as New Haven, which already had an affinity for celebrations; five years out was not too early to begin. Not surprisingly, then, the New Haven Bicentennial

Commission, which was created in April 1971, would eventually donate twelve thousand items to place in the archives at the New Haven Historical Society. Mayor Bartholomew Guida, the Elm City's second Italian American mayor, appointed W. Ogden Ross chairman, and by 1973, there was paid staff preparing for the event under Executive Director J'Lene Mayo. The commission was regional in scope, representing fifteen towns, though New Haven was once again at the center of the hub. New Haven's event planning was, in fact, the earliest in the state of Connecticut, and it's possible that some of the planners remembered the tercentenary in 1938. The New Haven Bicentennial Commission, run as a not-for-profit, managed its own visitor's center and published a newsletter, with many of its activities supported by grants from the Albie Booth Foundation, the Edgerton Foundation, the Hazen Foundation, the New Haven Foundation, the Connecticut Humanities Council, Connecticut Commission on the Arts and the National Endowment for the Arts. Like the tercentenary, the bicentennial committee finished its event with a profit.

In New Haven, the bicentennial began with a service at the grave of Roger Sherman at Grove Street Cemetery, where a red, white and blue wreath was placed on his grave by his descendants. A dedication ceremony to mark the renovation of city hall began at 12:30 p.m., with the nationwide ringing of bells at 2:00 p.m. City hall's bell tower had just received a new set of five bronze bells, and a "mass" of helium balloons were released from city hall when the bells were rung for two minutes, signifying two centuries of independence. Warren, Connecticut author and artist Eric Sloane and Eric Hatch of Litchfield were responsible for reviving the tradition of bell ringing on the Fourth of July, and Sloane himself came to New Haven to celebrate. Together the men had introduced a resolution that bells were to be rung every Fourth of July, which was put forward by Abraham Ribicoff in the Senate Congress (where it passed unanimously in 1963). The *Register* reported Sloane as saying, "My whole reason for being has been to reach into the past and find worthwhile things we've thrown away." In addition to the bells, the organist at Trinity Church, Stephen Loher, won a contest, and his composition was played across the nation.

The list of Fourth of July activities was considerable and included picnics, games, concerts, balls, a pageant, plays, films, dedications, memorials, a chicken barbecue, walking tours, a firemen's muster, a carnival, a tea for senior citizens, a reading of the Declaration of Independence and a special "Eighteenth Century Day." There are always complainers to be found, though; one person was reported as stating that "if there were more local activities, I would participate." Of course, fireworks in New Haven were the culminating event, though the bonfires lit around the city had most of the attention. Called an "epidemic" by the New Haven Fire Department, the *Register* reported on July 4 that "city fire, police and public works personnel scurried over the entire eastern half of the city Saturday night, putting out bonfires, clearing debris and being bombed by hand thrown salutes for their troubles." Large groups of neighborhood people, from Morris Cove to Bishops Woods School to Orange Street, lit and relit bonfires all night long. On Orange Street, New Haven firemen reported to the *Register* that until the police accompanied them, they refused to attend to the bonfires due to the number of fireworks that were being lit over their heads as they worked. On Quinnipiac Avenue, an abandoned boat shack went up in flames. With a sense of humor, New Haven police noted that "the usual run of Saturday night fights, domestic disputes and other activity had fallen off sharply, making the night a busy but bearable one."

The American bicentennial celebrations had a long-term impact on New Haven. In addition to the list of books published, historic sites in New Haven were given attention. A multiyear archaeological investigation of the Eli Whitney Armory site was supported, and the rebuilding of Black Rock Fort by Fort Hale Restorations Projects Inc., in partnership with the Redevelopment Agency and the Parks Department, occurred during the bicentennial. A Memorial Flag Court, the only one of its kind in New Haven, was landscaped at the fort, with a five-point star and a flagpole at each point of the star. The *Register* noted that the intent was to display the four different flags under which the fort was used, including the Cross of St. George (colonial), Grand Union (Revolutionary War), Star-Spangled Banner (War of 1812) and the thirty-four-star flag (Civil War). One of the flagpoles was dedicated to the memory of Charles Hervey Townshend, the sea captain who served in the Merchant Marines in the 1850s and then acted as the guardian of Fort Hale from circa 1865 to 1889.

Two of New Haven's Revolutionary War heroes became the subjects represented on the souvenir medallions. Designed by Clarence Doore, the two-sided image features Roger Sherman on the obverse and Nathan Hale on the reverse. Called a "strong competent rendering of Sherman," Doore's imagery pulled from both Ralph Earl's portrait and from John Trumbull's painting *Signing of the Declaration of Independence*; both works of art are always on display at the Yale University Art Gallery. The standing figure of Hale, arms bound, was also directly inspired by Yale's

Roger Sherman and Nathan Hale medallions. *Courtesy of the New Haven Museum. Photograph by Jessica Zielonka.*

art, specifically Bela Lyon Pratt's 1913 idealized statue located next to Connecticut Hall on Old Campus. While Moore's medium-relief carvings are, as stated in the New Haven bicentennial report, "strong [and] competent," they are renderings of works of art already in existence and are not terribly exciting. In other words, the zeal with which Americans felt toward the bicentennial is not translated into this visual statement, although the committee felt otherwise: "Our medallion promises to be not only a historic momento, but also a valid contribution to numismatic art in America." Doore had trained in sculpture in Boston and had completed two other commemorative medals before the New Haven commission, and it is strange that in a city filled with artists, an Elm City artist was not chosen for the commission.

Another lasting effect that the bicentennial celebrations had on New Haven centered on the work of the Ethnic Committee (calling itself "Twentieth Century Pilgrims"), which designed a daylong New World Festival. The festival featured tent displays of art, sculpture, exhibits, historic documents and a diverse series of live activities, all of which culminated with the musical *Purlie* on the performing arts stage at 5:00 p.m. before the fireworks. The festival also held an all-day family picnic. The New Haven Ethnic History exhibit highlighted the impact that Chinese, Lithuanians, Ukrainians, Jews, Italians, African Americans, Puerto Ricans, Polish, Germans, Italians, Armenians, Irish and Greeks had on the city. This information was also codified in the bicentennial souvenir book. For some, though, this was not enough. "There has been

New Haven Celebrates the Bicentennial, published by the New Haven Bicentennial Commission, 1976.

a lot to not celebrate concerning the minority groups," said Mercedes Chardia of Dwight Street in the *Register*; she worked at Yale-New Haven Hospital. This sentiment was repeated by a young man of twenty-three, Jose Hernandez, who said, "I'm a minority in this country. It's hard for me to feel any Bicentennial spirit, because the Spanish have been here for 400 years." Hernandez also commented on his lack of employment and how the bicentennial had not helped in that area either. While there were concerns and issues raised by New Haveners, the inclusion of the city's ethnic communities was built on traditions that dated to the middle of the nineteenth century and were further intensified during the tercentenary event. A full blossoming of this imperative reached its peak at New Haven's last celebration of the twentieth century, the 350th anniversary in 1988, from which the Ethnic Heritage Center was formed.

NEW HAVEN CELEBRATES
NEW HAVEN/NEW HAVEN 350, 1988

Once you get over the initial embarrassment of hanging around someone in Pilgrim shoes, it's kind of cute.

—New Haven Register, *April 24, 1988*

After reviewing two hundred years' worth of celebrations in New Haven, one statement heard repeatedly is that this or that event was going to be the biggest of them all. In the western world, without the practice of history—literary or visual—it really is difficult to remember what came before, so the *New Haven Register* quoting a planning committee member that the 350th anniversary was going to be the "biggest municipal birthday celebration in the history of Connecticut" is equal parts enthusiasm, showmanship and the kind of historical forgetfulness that David Lowenthal described in his book *The Past Is a Foreign Country* (published only a few years before New Haven's 350th anniversary). Even though the 350th celebration, called "New Haven Celebrates New Haven" or "New Haven 350," may not have been the biggest birthday celebration, it purposefully encompassed all that it could, spreading itself out from April to July and bringing the city's annual church festivals (such as the Feast of St. Anthony Festival, St. Michael's Outdoor Festival, the Santa Maria Maddalene festival and many other events) under the umbrella of New Haven Celebrates New Haven. Also included was "Israel in the Park" on Sunday, June 12; the fourth annual East Shore Day; the New Haven Jazz Festival; festival days on June 4 and 5; and on the Fourth of July itself, with an evening fireworks program named "Skyworks" that was, once again, called the "largest fireworks display in the history of Connecticut."

As had happened with past celebrations, it took the work of volunteer committee members to plan and manage the anniversary event, although this time, the leads were the city's print news publications, the *New Haven Register* and the *Independent*. No one was stepping up to the plate in terms of either sponsorship or leadership for the celebration, and in September 1987, the *Register* signed on to become the lead for the event. Clearly, it was new territory for the newsmen and women, as Bill Cotter, marketing manager for the paper, said, "It was a scary thing…in September everyone got together in the *Register*'s community rooms and broke up into committee groups. I swore it would never be pulled off." The City of New Haven contributed, too, in the form of Robert (Bob) Gregson, a municipal employee who was given

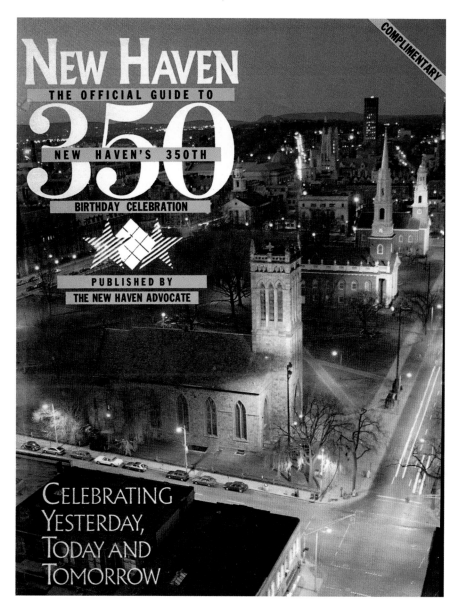

New Haven 350th birthday program, published by the *New Haven Advocate. Courtesy of Joseph Taylor.*

"on loan" to the planning committee. Cotter gave Gregson the credit for "running the whole show," which he stated was done to "to demonstrate the paper's commitment to the city." With a different insight, Cynthia Savo, the publisher of the *Independent* and co-chair of the New Haven 350 Committee, gave her rationale for supporting the event:

New Haven's 350th...carries a much greater potential: for New Haven as a whole—not just politicians and business executives—to construct a new definition of civic pride, by examining our warts along with our virtues and strengthening the ties of community in a city of many traditions...in addition to giving people a good time—a worthy goal on a birthday—these projects enable members of a diverse and too often divided community to learn more about each other and to get back in touch with their own history.

New Haven's history was again called to action, and the planning committee chose the slogan "Where Tradition Meets the Future" as the winning entry in a contest in which 3,200 people entered and vied for the $350 award. As the repository for the histories of New Haven, the city's museums were highlighted for the first time during an anniversary celebration—from Saturday, May 14, through May 22, "Museum Magic: A Celebration of New Haven's Museums" (which included some no longer in existence, such as the Gowie-Normand House and the National Art Museum of Sport). There was also a Powder House Day Brawl (dance), where many people dressed in costume; local civic leaders played the roles of John Davenport, Theophilus Eaton, Benedict Arnold and the Three Judges. The semi-centennial medallion produced for the event by artist Paul Lantuch is another reworking of Hezekiah Auger's 1838 design. Like the 250th medal, John Davenport gets the credit as "Founder of New Haven," but here his flock is nowhere to be seen. On the reverse is Auger's reproduced design, updated with I-95 and the connectors, providing the transportation routes in and out of the city. The Three Churches on the Green are also gone, replaced by the city's twentieth-century skyline. The museum- and history-based programs of New Haven 350 were overshadowed by the real emphasis of the event: the theme of diversity. Gregson was quoted in the June 2, 1988 edition of the *Independent* as saying, "The underlying idea is to take all this incredible diversity and bring it back to its roots, back to the Green where it all began."

Thus, during the festival days, there was a "Communidiversity Day '88" and an "International Heritage Tent" on the Green, showcasing "Something from Everybody," with exhibitions by the city's ethnic groups and demonstrations of the preparation of ethnic foods. The theme of ethnic diversity was shared by Yale University, which sponsored a "Concert of Celebration," a musical program in eight sections by Fenno Heath and Thomas Duffy (constructed for Woosley Hall), in which New Haven's history was traced from 1836 onward. The concert organizers worked local

New Haven 350th galvanos (electrolytic casts), Paul Lantuch. *Courtesy of the New Haven Museum. Photograph by Jessica Zielonka.*

citizens into the performance during the sixth section, titled "Strength in Diversity." Mayor Biagio DiLieto, Yale president Benno Schmidt and Lloyd Richardson, the dean of the Yale School of Drama, were the narrators. This performance was not unlike the Woolsey Hall concert held during the tercentenary in which diversity was also the theme. For the first time in New Haven, in regards to the theme of diversity, the idea included "accessibility." Thus, the planning committee put in place volunteers to assist people in wheelchairs, those with special needs and the elderly. Clearly, the thinking behind the soon-to-be-passed Americans with Disabilities Act (1990) was already becoming a part of American culture.

In all, it was reported that seventy exhibitors, eighty performers and twenty-four food vendors attended New Haven 350, but the most important impact this semi-centennial had on the city was its role as a booster and generator for multiple new organizations, some of which joined together as the Ethnic Heritage Center, today located on the campus of Southern Connecticut State University. Ethnic societies, churches, schools and festivals had been a large part of New Haven's identity since the mid-nineteenth century, and the participation of such groups in the city's celebrations has been demonstrated in this book. But it was not until the late twentieth century that specific groups began to develop their own historical organizations, with the purpose of recording oral history, collecting archival documents and historic objects and offering educational programs in support of language, culture and history. In New Haven, the Jewish Historical Society was formed during the bicentennial year, although the Young Men's Hebrew Association (the precursor to the Jewish Community Center of Greater New Haven) had been in existence in the Elm City since 1912. By the spring of 1988, the Jewish Historical Society, the Connecticut Afro-American Historical Society (the precursor to the current African-American Historical Society, founded in 1971) and the Italian-American Historical Society (founded 1979) were making plans for a "multi-ethnic historical center."

As reported in the December 1, 1988 edition of the *Independent*, there were other groups in formation too: "This 350th celebration year of New Haven has seen the formation of new city Irish, Hispanic, Women's and Labor History groups, with a Greek group in the wings." There was also talk of an American Museum of Theatre (not surprising, given New Haven's rich theater history) and a Hispanic Historical Society. Some of these came to fruition, some did not and others that came into being no longer exist. Some at the New Haven Colony Historical Society, the precursor to the New Haven Museum, were not pleased about the enlarging of institutions in collecting New Haven history, criticizing in the *Register* the use of the term "ethnic" and arguing "would it not be more prudent to support the effort of the institutions that have done the job for a long time and have done it well?"

One of the other illuminating pieces that came out of New Haven 350 was the collective statement made by the city's independent business owners. The *Register* ran a special advertising section six times over the course of the year titled "A Declaration of New Haven Independents" and which stated, "Independence, Ingenuity, Innovation. We, the undersigned, as owners of independent New Haven businesses, are proud of those three words. They symbolize the tradition that has set New Haven apart for three and a half centuries and will continue to set us apart for centuries to come." This is a timely sentiment in 2013, and it continues to shape the city, as New Haven, while losing historic independents, also manages to gain many more at the same time. About the most important advice anyone can give for designing future anniversary celebrations in New Haven comes from the 1988 semi-

Coming Out Party for the Ethnic Historical Archives, program. Joel Wasserman, the president of the Jewish Historical Society, was the spokesman and primary mover behind the effort to create the collaborative. Khalid Lum, a reporter for the *New Haven Independent*, provided press, though the collaborative received notice in the Sunday, April 17, 1988 issue of the *New York Times* as well. *Courtesy of the Ethnic Heritage Center. Photograph by Jessica Zielonka.*

centennial. As Bob Gregson said, "It worked because the whole community got behind it. Just a tremendous amount of people have gotten together to pull this off...it's going to be a monster celebration."

TREASURES FROM LATE TWENTIETH-CENTURY NEW HAVEN

It is telling that the treasures saved from late twentieth-century New Haven are different from everything we have seen thus far. This is true both in who owned the objects originally and in who owns them now. That is, these objects were owned by the working classes, and it is in the late twentieth century that the lives of people outside the white, politically powerful and elite became of interest to scholars. This reflects the great paradigm shift in the practice of writing history in the twentieth century. The "new history" was about everyone in society, and for the first time, the lives of women, gays, Native Americans, laborers and the disabled, among others, were integrated into academic scholarship and museum work. In New Haven, this work was most active under the ethnic heritage societies already discussed. However, far fewer objects exist in New Haven museum collections from the second half of the twentieth century. Some of this is due to the changing nature of our stuff—people no longer write letters since they send digital text messages—but there is also the lingering problem of value. When space is at a premium (as it is in all of New Haven's collecting institutions), what gets saved and what gets tossed? The questions, then, become who is actively collecting New Havens materials from the turn of the twenty-first century, and what kind of history will be written without access to our material lives?

Oak Street sign, metal. One simple pressed sheet of metal with two short words agitates even today, more than fifty years after the neighborhood was razed to make way for urban redevelopment plans that were never fully realized. The Oak Street neighborhood was composed of tenements filled with Jewish, Italian and other immigrant families and their local stores. In 2012, the area was once again in the news, as new municipal plans for development were debated. *Courtesy of the Jewish Historical Society of Greater New Haven. Photograph by Greg Bianchini.*

International Ladies Garment Workers Union dress. This dress, made of fabric stamped with the International Ladies Garment Works Union/AFLCIO label, may have been worn by a proud worker to a Labor Day parade or demonstration. Though less than fifty years old (and thus, in some circles, barely qualifying for "historic" status), dramatic changes in the American context of manufacturing, business practices and the weakening of unions at the end of the twentieth century means that this object has become a relic of a time when unions were a world unto themselves, with weekly newspapers, musical programs and trips to out-of-state conventions and meetings. *Courtesy of the Greater New Haven Labor History Association, Garment Workers Collection. Photograph by Jessica Zielonka.*

EVERYBODY OUT ON TUESDAY!

Protest Meeting on the Green at Noon

Stop Jailing the Teachers!

It is a disgrace that the New Haven teachers are being jailed.

It is part of an all-out union-busting campaign.

The Board of Education is carrying the ball for every anti-union employer in the area.

This barbaric treatment of our teachers is a threat to our entire labor movement.

TUESDAY AT NOON WE DEMONSTRATE OUR SUPPORT!

To demonstrate labor's united support, 147 leaders of the Greater New Haven Central Labor Council (AFL-CIO) and Independent Unions call for a Giant Protest Rally:

TUESDAY, NOV. 25, AT NOON ON THE NEW HAVEN GREEN

Everybody who is shocked and angry at what they are doing to our teachers is urged to attend.

The jailings threaten our own jobs, our wage standards and our unions.

EVERYBODY OUT ON THE GREEN ON TUESDAY!

Issued by: The Greater New Haven Central Labor Council
30 Hazel Terrace, Woodbridge, Conn.

12

Teachers' strike poster, New Haven Federation of Teachers Local 933 Collection. New Haven remains a center for unionized workers as both the support staffs of Yale University and Yale–New Haven Hospital, the city's largest employers, and the New Haven Public School system are unionized. Union struggles were a large part of the New Haven landscape in the 1970s. Between 1970 and 1975, there with three teachers' strikes that brought an end to the tenure of Mayor Bartholomew Guida. For ignoring a Superior Court injunction, ninety teachers were jailed in Bridgeport and Niantic and at the National Guard's Camp Hartell in Windsor Locks. *Courtesy of the Greater New Haven Labor History Association. Photograph by Jessica Zielonka.*

Black Panthers "Free Clothing Program" flyer. The Black Panthers had a significant presence in the Elm City in the late 1960s and 1970s. While the Panthers pressed for greater equality and assistance for black Americans, often using militaristic tactics, they also sponsored local grass-roots community programs such as providing breakfast for young students and published a newspaper called *The Crow*, sponsored by black-owned businesses. The Black Power movement reached its climax in New Haven when Founder Bobby Seale was brought to trial for the murder of party member Alex Rackley. This led to the May Day 1970 protest on the Green, where many Yale students were involved. *Courtesy of the African-American Historical Society. Photograph by Jessica Zielonka.*

Lender's Bagels bank truck, accession #05-84. Founded in New Haven by Harry Lender in 1927, Lender's Bagels was one of the first bagel bakeries outside of New York City and used strategic marketing efforts, later called the "bagelizing of America," to introduce frozen bagels to supermarket moms in the 1950s. Bagel imagery was even appropriated for Senator Joe Lieberman's campaigns: one pin features his face inserted into the bagel hole, with the inscription, "A bagel in every pot." This bank truck is meant to evoke Lender's beginnings delivering bagels for the Saturday evening/Sunday morning rush. In 1984, Lender's was the largest producer of bagels in the world and was sold to Kraft Foods Inc. *Courtesy of the Jewish American Historical Society of Greater New Haven. Photograph by Jessica Zielonka.*

CONCLUSION

Now that the important anniversary celebrations in New Haven have been identified and described, we can begin to see patterns specific to New Haven emerge in a constant recycling of ideals, memory and desire. These patterns feed the identity of the city and generally emphasize a desire to remember the past for perceived qualities such as sound moral leadership while, at the same time, creating a future embodied in the evolving concept of progress. Again, though, we must remember that the celebrations highlighted in this book existed in a much richer landscape of events that were equally meaningful for participants. For example, a metal souvenir coin produced in 1934 for the 100th anniversary of St. John Roman Catholic Church (a site recently back in the spotlight due to the discovery of the church's original cemetery, which is today under the entrance to Yale–New Haven Hospital) demonstrates one special community out of hundreds that existed in New Haven.

While the number of churches, synagogues and temples in the Elm City is one potential area of investigation for celebrations and events, a study of specific ethnic celebrations and parades, such as those of New Haven's Italian American community, would also prove enlightening. Here again we have the objects to remind us of this tradition—the banner collection of the Italian-American Historical Society has much to tell us. Another important area of inquiry concerns the use of New Haven for military drills, parades and encampments. Many photographs attesting to the Elm City's role have been published, but a thorough study tracing this history

St. John's Roman Catholic Church centennial medal (1834/1934). Evidence of this church's history became of interest again in 2011–12, when human remains were discovered where Yale–New Haven Hospital was building a new expanded entrance. The hospital sits on the old Christ Church/St. John the Evangelist property, and while the second church building on site was eventually demolished, the bodies of church members buried in the cemetery right outside its door had been forgotten. A photograph showing the cemetery and other archival materials have helped local historians piece the story together. *Courtesy of Joseph Taylor. Photograph by Jessica Zielonka.*

remains to be done. We have also seen that because New Haven is the home of Yale University, the campus and downtown intertwined, Yale's own celebrations were very much a part of the Elm City landscape too. The impact of Yale celebrations on New Haven was palpable. Also integrated into the calendar of yearly celebrations was Flag Day and Memorial Day, both of which offered opportunities for parades and fireworks. The liberty pole on the New Haven Green, installed in the eighteenth century, continued to be a focal point for celebration.

This book has categorized some of the types of celebratory events in New Haven over the past two hundred years or more, and we have learned about who was involved and why. One lingering question remains: who

Right: Gara di Benemerenze banner, 3' x 2', 1938. This "first place" banner may have been used in parades and/or was taken to meetings at other Italian American clubs. The Italian-American Historical Society of Connecticut has five different banners in its collection, two of which (including this one) demonstrates Italian American support for Benito Mussolini before direct American involvement in World War II. Small busts of Mussolini (the historical society owns one) and other inexpensively produced and thus widely available objects would also have been displayed in local homes. The *Corriere d'America* was an Italian American newspaper and thus probably a sponsor of the event in which this banner was won. *Courtesy of the Italian American Historical Society of Connecticut. Photograph by Jessica Zielonka.*

Below: Yale bicentennial celebration, photograph, circa 1901. *Courtesy of Joseph Taylor.*

was included and who was excluded in these events? I spent some time discussing the representation of Native Americans in New Haven and the ethnic groups that have been a part of New Haven society since the mid-nineteenth century, but what about women and the black community, both of whom have long presences in the city but seem to be missing from these celebrations? It is not a stretch to say that these celebrations, more closely aligned with the ruling elite of the city than not, summarize different but equally damaging attitudes toward these two groups of people.

We have seen that sometimes women did participate in New Haven celebrations, marching in the parades, attending church services and serving on planning committees. But these efforts received far less attention in the newspapers. From some of the comments read, it becomes clear that in terms of celebrations, women are most often noted in relation to the concept of beauty—or lack of it. As an example, the *New Haven Evening Register* reported on July 3, 1879, that "it will be difficult…to find a good spot to see the procession; or a good looking woman over thirty," though two days later the paper followed with, "The most attractive features [of the parade], however, was the wagon containing a pyramid of young ladies, who, by contrast, followed a wagon full of women of 1779." Humor aside, this continued right through the early twentieth century, when the *Register* published a photograph of a mostly male crowd ogling women on stage in bathing suits at the 1938 Tercentenary Exposition. Clearly, women could be personifications of Lady Liberty, Quinnipiac Indians or bathing beauties, but the written history of New Haven is a male affair. Important women in twentieth-century New Haven history such as Augusta Lewis Troup or Constance Baker Motley came along too late to be codified into celebrations, as were male Puritans, revolutionaries and industrialists.

This is in contrast to the almost complete lack of engagement the black community received from the planning committees of New Haven celebrations. As with women, there are examples of black participation, but this was due distinctly to the Afro-American Committee during the bicentennial, which sponsored a play about the *Amistad*. Nothing is said at all about African Americans or other people of color during any of the previous celebrations (this is also at odds with the many times that Cinque and the *Amistad* were celebrated in murals from the 1930s). The book *New Haven Illustrated* offers one reading of this state of affairs, the idea that "[m]ost people seemed indifferent, at best, to the aspirations of the black community which formed the lowest socioeconomic group in the city." It's not as though African Americans were new to New Haven—Theophilus Eaton had two black slaves with him when he came to New Haven. But clearly, the black community was not considered to be part of the New Haven story. Many American cities had parades in which whites appeared in blackface, some reenacting scenes of slavery, and though some in New Haven did perform in "redface," nothing appears in the newspapers about the use of blackface in parades, nor the reenacting of scenes of black life, in the Elm City.

In the end, many celebrations have ceased, and others have come close to ending due to the changing desires and needs in society. Looking at these important cultural rituals offers us another route into the study of New Haven history, well suited to an integration of textual and visual materials. With every milestone the city reaches, there remains the opportunity to look behind and choose what might lie ahead. As the *New Haven Evening Register* reported at the 250th anniversary in 1888, "What New Haven will be two hundred and fifty years hence depends largely upon what we do for New Haven today."

THE TERCENTENARY QUIZ

HOW MUCH DO YOU KNOW ABOUT NEW HAVEN?

This quiz was published by the Free Public Library of New Haven in 1938. Quiz participants had to go to one of the branch libraries to get the answers. In 1938, there were seven branches of the New Haven Public Library (Davenport Branch at 261 Portsea Street, Dixwell Branch at 555 Dixwell Avenue, Fair Haven Branch at 182 Grand Avenue, Mitchell Memolrial Branch at 37 Harrison Street, Farnam House Branch at 198 Hamilton Street, Nathan Hale Branch at 480 Townsend Avenue and Scranton Branch at 81 Scranton Avenue). The questions remain challenging for all but the most ardent history students. New Haven teachers could update and use this quiz. Judging from the responses marked on the original, the subject of history was not the strong suit of this participant.

1. The area of New Haven Green is about:

- 16 acres
- 29 acres
- 6 acres

2. The first settlers came to New Haven on the ship:

- *Welcome*
- *Hector*
- *The Phantom Ship*

3. The hero who demands the keys of the Powder House on Foot Guard Day is:

- Benedict Arnold
- Nathan Hale
- George Washington

4. One of the following statements describes the height of West Rock in comparison with the Empire State Building:

- They are about the same height
- West Rock is higher
- The Empire State Building is about three times as high

5. The trade-mark that you see on door locks is:

- Winchester
- Sargent
- Gilbert

6. Judges' Cave is situated:

- On West Rock
- On East Rock
- In Grove Street Cemetery

7. One of these famous inventors was *not* connected with New Haven:

- Charles Goodyear
- Eli Whitney
- Thomas Edison
- Eli Whitney Blake

8. An Indian chief who signed the deed of sale of New Haven was:

- Momauguin
- Quinnipiac
- Sitting Bull

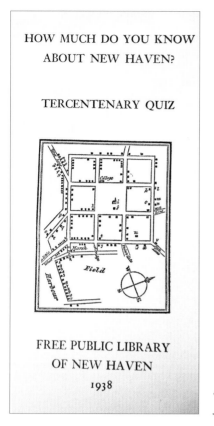

HOW MUCH DO YOU KNOW
ABOUT NEW HAVEN?

TERCENTENARY QUIZ

FREE PUBLIC LIBRARY
OF NEW HAVEN
1938

Tercentenary quiz. *Courtesy of the Whitney Library, New Haven Museum.*

9. The first mayor of New Haven was:

- Elihu Yale
- Theophilus Eaton
- Roger Sherman

10. Only one of the following statements is true:

- Noah Webster wrote his dictionary in a house on College Street
- Center Church is the oldest church in the city
- New Haven is the largest city in Connecticut

APPENDIX

CHRONOLOGY OF MAJOR NEW HAVEN CELEBRATIONS

1781   peace celebration (end to the hostilities of the American Revolution)

1783   peace celebration (Treaty of Paris/American Revolution)

1784   (Fourth of July) celebration of the incorporation of the city of New Haven

1788   (Fourth of July) celebration of the adoption of the federal Constitution

1814   (Fourth of July) during the War of 1812

1815   peace celebration (War of 1812)

1826   (Fourth of July) American jubilee in New Haven

1838   (April) New Haven second centennial

1865   (April) peace celebration (Civil War)/death of Lincoln

1876   (Fourth of July) American centennial

1879   (Fourth of July) centennial celebration of the evacuation/invasion of New Haven

1884   (Fourth of July) centennial celebration of the incorporation of the city of New Haven

1887   (June 17) Monument Day (dedication of the Soldiers and Sailors Monument)

1888   (April) Founders' Day (New Haven's 250th anniversary)

1892   (October 11) Columbus Day 400th anniversary celebration

1901   Yale University bicentennial

1905   (April 24) Powder House Day

1912   (September 19–21) New Haven Week

1916   (October 21) Yale Pageant, 200th anniversary of Yale College coming to New Haven

1918   (November 16) peace celebration (end of World War I)

1935   Connecticut tercentennial celebration

1938   (April) New Haven tercentennial

1945   peace celebration (end of World War II)

1976   (Fourth of July) American bicentennial

1988   (April–July) New Haven celebrates New Haven (350th anniversary)

1992   500th anniversary of Columbus

2001   Yale University tercentennial

REFERENCES

BOOKS AND ARTICLES

Bacon, Leonard. *Thirteen Historical Discourses on the Completion of Two Hundred Years, from the Beginning of the First Church in New Haven with an Appendix*. New Haven, CT: Durrie and Peck, 1839.

Barber, J.W. *History and Antiquities of New Haven, Conn. from Its Earliest Settlement to the Present Time*, New Haven, CT: self-published, 1831.

Benton, Tim, ed. *Understanding Heritage and Memory*. Manchester, UK: Open University, 2010.

Brown, Elizabeth Mills. *New Haven: A Guide to Architecture and Urban Design*. New Haven, CT: Yale University Press, 1976.

Burstein, Andrew. *America's Jubilee*. New York: Alfred A. Knopf, 2001.

Bushman, Richard L. *The Refinement of America: Persons, Houses, Cities*. New York: Vintage Books, 1992.

Collier, Christopher. *Roger Sherman: Puritan Politician*, New Haven Colony Monograph Series, Volume Two, 1976.

Conn, Steven. *Do Museums Still Need Objects?* Philadelphia: University of Pennsylvania Press, 2010.

Corrigan, David. "New Haven Mourns George Washington." *Journal of the New Haven Colony Historical Society* 26, no. 1 (Spring 1979): 3–20.

Costello, A.E. *History of the New Haven Police Department*. New Haven, CT: Relief Book Publishing Company, 1892.

Finlay, Victoria. *Color: A Natural History of the Palette*. New York: Random House Trade Paperbacks, 2002.

Glassberg, David. *American Historical Pageantry: The Uses of Tradition in the Early Twentieth Century*. Chapel Hill: University of North Carolina Press, 1990.

Hegel, Richard. *Nineteenth Century Historians of New Haven.* Hamden, CT: Archon Books, 1972.

Hogan, Neil. *Moments in New Haven Labor History.* New Haven, CT: Greater New Haven Labor History Association, 2004.

Hornstein, Harold, ed. *New Haven Celebrates the Bicentennial, Commemorative Book.* New Haven, CT: Eastern Press, 1976.

The Hundredth Anniversary of the City of New Haven with the Oration by Thomas Rutherford Bacon, Also a Paper on New Haven in 1784 by Franklin Bowditch Dexter. New Haven, CT: Norris G. Osborn and Burton Mansfield, 1885.

Jaffee, David. *A New Nation of Goods: The Material Culture of Early America.* Philadelphia: University of Pennsylvania Press, 2010.

Kingsley, William L. *1638–1888: The Historic Forces Which Gave Rise to Puritanism, an Address in the Occasion of the 250th Anniversary of the Settlement of New Haven.* N.p., 1888.

Kirby, John B., Jr. "New Haven's 1783 Peace Flag." *Journal of the New Haven Colony Historical Society* 31, no. 3 (Summer 1985): 20–24.

Kubler, George. *The Shape of Time: Remarks on the History of Things.* New Haven, CT: Yale University Press, 1962.

Leeney, Robert J. Elms. *Arms & Ivy: New Haven in the Twentieth Century.* Montgomery, AL: Community Communications Inc., 2000.

Malia, Peter J. *Visible Saints: West Haven, Connecticut, 1648–1798.* Monroe: Connecticut Press, 2009.

Matheson, Susan B. *Art for Yale: A History of the Yale University Art Gallery.* New Haven, CT: Yale University Art Gallery, 2001.

Menta, John. *The Quinnipiac: Cultural Conflict in Southern New England.* Yale University Publications in Anthropology No. 86. New Haven, CT: Yale University, 2003.

Mininberg, Mark J. *Saving New Haven: John W. Murphy Faces the Crisis of the Great Depression.* New Haven, CT: Fine Arts Publications, 1988.

Moynihan, Joan, and Neil Hogan. *New Haven's St. Patrick's Day Parade.* Charleston, SC: Arcadia Publishing, 2006.

O'Brien, Jean M. *Firsting and Lasting: Writing Indians Out of Existence in New England.* Minneapolis: University of Minnesota Press, 2010.

Ransom, David F. "Connecticut's Monumental Epoch: A Survey of Civil War Memorials." *Connecticut Historical Society Bulletin* 58 (1993).

Sletcher, Michael. *New Haven, from Puritanism to the Age of Terrorism.* Charleston, SC: Arcadia Publishing, 2004.

Starbuck, David. "Archaeological Research at the Eli Whitney Factory Site." *Journal of the New Haven Colony Historical Society* 25, no. 1 (Summer 1997): 27.

Ulrich, Laurel Thatcher. *The Age of Homespun: Objects and Stories in the Creation of an American Myth.* New York: Vintage Books, 2001.

Wildersheim, William A. "The New Haven Grays." *Journal of the New Haven Colony Historical Society* 26, no. 1 (Spring 1979): 21–31.

PAMPHLETS, EXHIBITION CATALOGUES AND ARCHIVAL MATERIALS

American Revolution Bicentennial Advisory Commission (New Haven edition) newsletter (Fall 1973, Winter 1974 and Fall 1974).

The Bicentennial Radio Series, "New Haven: The Earliest Years" and "New Haven: The Revolutionary Generation," The New Haven Bicentennial Commission, New Haven: The Harty Press, 1976.

Ethnic Heritage Center. *An Ethnic History of New Haven.* New Haven, CT: self-published, 2009. http://www.criscoladesign.com/pdfs/ehc_census.pdf.

Exercises at the Unveiling of the Monument to Adjutant William Campbell. New Haven, CT: Monument Committee, 1891.

Handbook of the Centennial Exhibition of American and Revolutionary Relics. New Haven, CT: Punderson & Crisand, 1875.

Joel Wasserman Ethnic Heritage Center Records, Ethnic Heritage Center, New Haven, Connecticut.

New England Celebrates: Spectacle, Commemoration and Festivity. Dublin Seminar for New England Folklife Annual Proceedings. Deerfield, MA: Historic Deerfield, 2000.

New Haven Bicentennial Commission Records, 1971–76, MSS B15, Whitney Library, New Haven Museum, New Haven, Connecticut.

New Haven Colony Historical Society. *An Exhibition of New Haven Silver.* New Haven, CT: self-published, 1967.

The New Haven State House with Some Account of the Green, New Haven: H. Peck & G.H. Coe, 1889.

New Haven Tercentenary Records, 1938, MSS B3, Whitney Library, New Haven Museum, New Haven, Connecticut.

New Haven 350 Cultural and Historical Association Records, MSS 235, Whitney Library, New Haven Museum, New Haven, Connecticut.

Prendergast, William J., comp. *Two Hundred Years: The Second Company Governor's Footguard, 1775–1975.* Deep River, CT: New Era Printing Company Inc., 1975.

Proceedings at the Public Opening, September 28, 1893, of the New Haven Colony Historical Society Building Erected by Henry F. English as a Memorial of James E and Caroline F. English. New Haven, CT: Tuttle, Morehouse & Taylor, 1893.

Proceedings in Commemoration of the Settlement of the Town of New Haven. N.p., April 25, 1888.

United States Bicentennial Committee Records, Yale University, 1970–77, RU 714, Manuscripts and Archives, Sterling Memorial Library, Yale University.

NEWSPAPERS

Columbian Weekly Register. November 26, 1864; March 11, April 15, April 22, June 10 and July 1, 1865; July 1 and 8, 1876. News Bank, American's Historical Newspapers, www.infoweb.newsbank.com.

Connecticut Courant. July 14, 1788. News Bank, American's Historical Newspapers, www.infoweb.newsbank.com.

Connecticut Herald. February 14, 21 and 28, March 7 and July 14, 1815; July 4 and 11, 1826; April 22, 1865. Connecticut State Library, microfilm, and News Bank, American's Historical Newspapers, www.infoweb.newsbank.com.

Connecticut Journal. July 17, 1776; November 8 and 15, 1781; April 24 and May 1, 1783; June 27 and July 4, 5, 10 and 11, 1814; February 13, 20 and 27, 1815. News Bank, American's Historical Newspapers, www.infoweb. newsbank.com.

Daily Herald. April 23, 24, 26 and 27, 1838. Connecticut State Library, microfilm.

New-Haven Columbian Register. April 21 and 28, 1838. Whitney Library, New Haven Museum.

New Haven Evening Register. July 1 and 5, 1884; March 28, April 12–13, 16–19, 21, 23–26 and 28 and May 14, 17 and 26, 1888; April 24, 1905; November 11–12 and 16, 1918; May 8 and 10, 1945; August 14–15, 1945. News Bank, American's Historical Newspapers, www.infoweb.newsbank.com.

New Haven Independent. March 24, June 2, June 9 and December 1, 1988, Ethnic Heritage Center, New Haven, Connecticut.

New Haven Journal Courier. April 23, 25 and 26, 1938.

New Haven Register. May 6, 1974; April 27, 1975; May 25, 1975; July 4 and 6, 1976; May 7, 1978; May 6, 1984; February 16, March 23 and April 24, 1988; August 29, 1989. New Haven Public Library, microfilm, and the Ethnic Heritage Center, New Haven, Connecticut.

New Haven Sunday Register. November 17, 1918.

Pinto, Amanda. "Society Planning to Sell Land, Move Historic Campbell Monument." *New Haven Register,* July 19, 2010.

———. "West Haven Historical Society Drops Plan to Sell Land with Campbell Monument." *New Haven Register,* September 18, 2010.

Saturday Chronicle (New Haven edition). April 13, 1907; April 19, 1913. Whitney Library, New Haven Museum.

ABOUT THE AUTHOR AND PHOTOGRAPHER

Laura A. Macaluso has degrees in art history from Southern Connecticut State University, Syracuse University's Florence program, and is currently a doctoral candidate at Salve Regina University, Newport, Rhode Island. She has worked as an administrator, curator and grant writer for the National Park Service, the City of New Haven's Department of Arts, Culture & Tourism and several historic sites, museums and park organizations. In 2008–9, she held a Fulbright at the Swaziland National Museum in southern Africa, and the following year, she was project manager for Swaziland's first Ambassadors Fund for Cultural Preservation grant, from the U.S. Department of State. She lives in Lynchburg, Virginia, with her husband and an old cat.

Jessica Zielonka is a recent graduate of the photography program at Southern Connecticut State University. She has always enjoyed photographing people, as well as the objects and artifacts that are a part of their everyday lives. Jess loves experimenting with food and makes a mean chocolate cookie. She currently lives in New Haven, Connecticut.

Visit us at
www.historypress.net

....

This title is also available as an e-book.